How to Draw

ADVANCED

NeoPopRealism

INK images

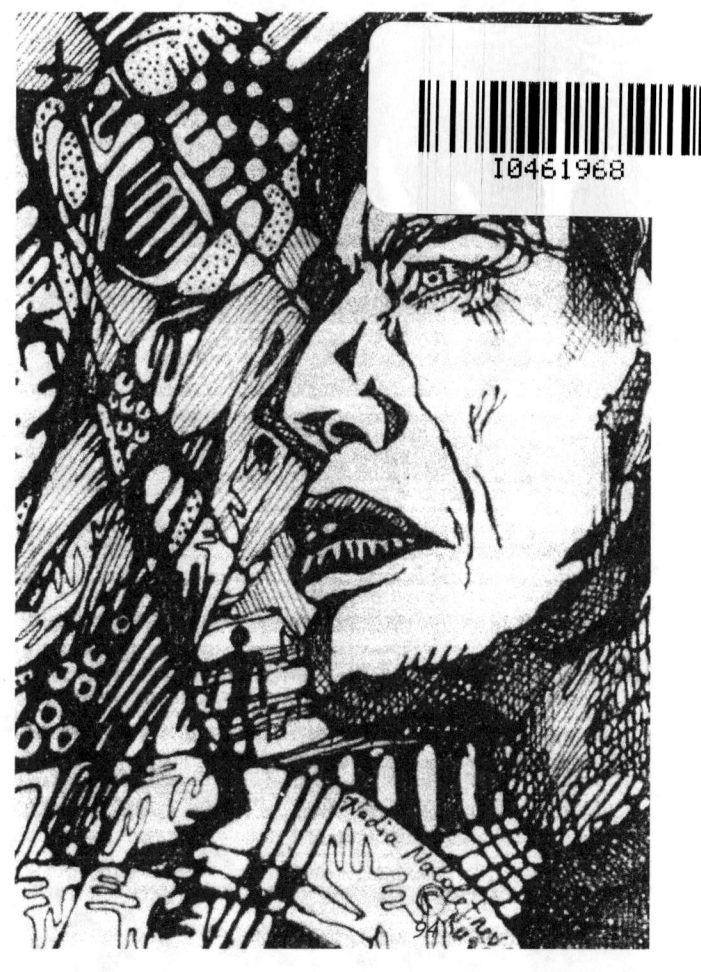

NADIA RUSS

NeoPopRealism PRESS

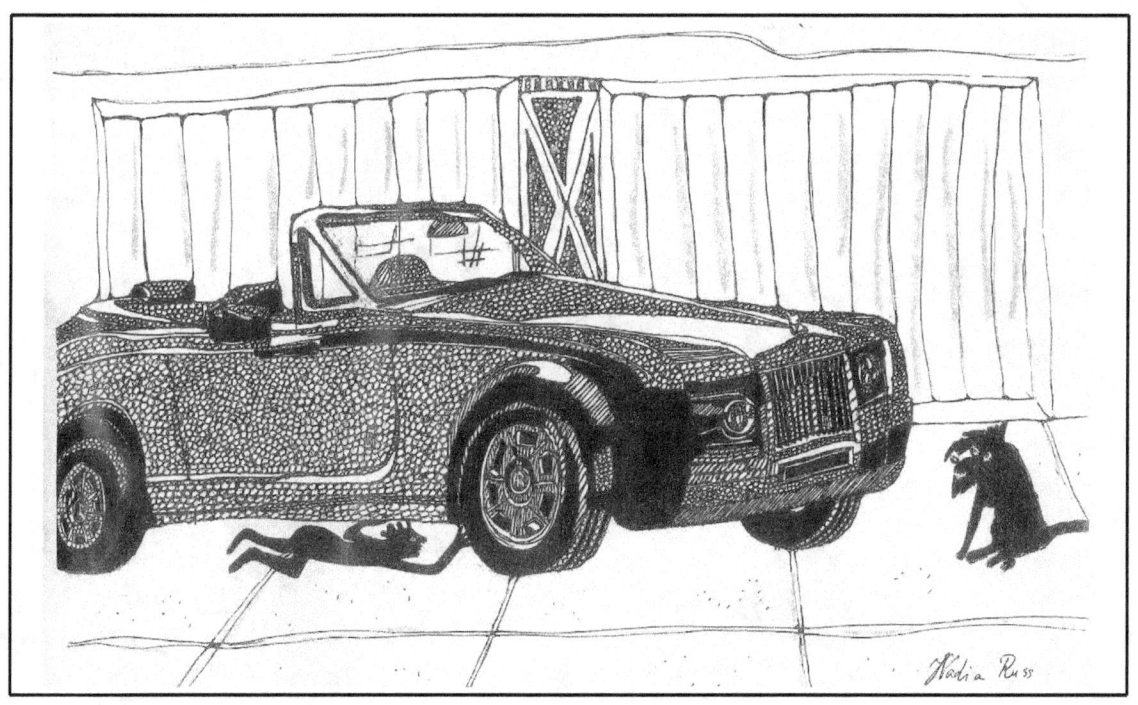

Nadia Russ, *Rolls Royce Convertible,* Ink on paper, mixed media, 11"x17", 2006
Collection of MOYA, Museum of Young Art, Vienna, Austria

How to draw
ADVANCED
NeoPopRealism
INK images

NADIA RUSS
NeoPopRealism PRESS

First published in 2011 by NeoPopRealism PRESS
PO BOX 366
New York, NY 10013

NeopoprealismPress@mail.com

"*How to Draw Advanced NeoPopRealism Ink Images*" by Nadia RUSS (aka Nadejda Maloletneva)
Illustrations by Nadia Russ

Front cover images: "*Mick Jagger*" by Nadia Russ, ink on paper, 1994 and "*Queen of Magic*" by Nadia Russ, acrylic on canvas, 1997.
Back cover image: "*Amy Winehouse*" by Nadia Russ, ink on paper, 2011.

Published in the United States of America
Language: English

ISBN-13: 9780615569758
ISBN-10: 0615569757

11 12 13 14 15   10 9 8 7 6 5 4 3 2 1

This book teaches how to draw advanced NeoPopRealism ink images.

www.neopoprealism.org

CONTENT

INTRODUCTION

NeoPopRealism ink drawing concept was created by Nadia Russ in 1989. It was an experiment. She was trying to connect to the Universe and let the Universe use her as a Conductor when she created her drawings. She didn't want to follow any other artists' achievements, she decided to create absolutely new art form, like Picasso (Cubism), Dali (Surrealism), Andy Warhol (Pop Art) and a few other worldwide known artists had done.

Nadia Russ took her ink pen and began to draw a flowing line that turned into shapes, figures, often faces. Then, some sections (or all), that appeared, she filled with the repetitive patterns. She never uses eraser because if a mistake made, it disappears with the following repetitive patterns that balance the whole composition. Her work was unique, no one did anything like this before.

Later, January 4, 2003, Nadia Russ created a word NeoPopRealism and internationally announced new style of visual arts.

Сако САСАДЗАВА
(Япония)

ПОЕЗДКА
К МОРЮ

1

Прочитав короткое письмо, Садахико Когава подумал, что это, наверное, какой-то новый рекламный трюк. Потом решил, что, пожалуй, дело не в этом. Едва открывшемуся новому отелю на берегу моря не было никакой необходимости применять такие методы по отношению к нему, Садахико Когаве. Он не был ни богат, ни знаменит. В свои тридцать три года он работал в популярном журнале, но всего лишь младшим редактором. Хотя денежных затруднений он не испытывал, все же доход едва давал ему возможность удовлетворять все свои желания и желания жены и троих детей. Если бы отель преследовал рекламные цели, то письмо послали бы кому-нибудь из заметных людей.

Письмо было написано элегантным почерком и немного странным.

«Хотя это и может показаться неожиданным, я пишу, чтобы сообщить о своем сердечном приглашении. Я буду очень рада, если вы согласитесь провести весьма приятную ночь в одном из лучших номеров отеля «Того Кавадзу», на побережье Кавадзу — это на восточном берегу полуострова Идзу. Если вы примете мое приглашение, пожалуйста, приезжайте в отель к пяти вечера в субботу, 1 августа.

Будьте любезны показать это письмо служащему за стойкой регистрации. Вас отведут в комнату. Я взяла на себя смелость присовокупить к письму деньги на дорогу. Море»

В конверте были также две бумажки по десять тысяч иен. Возможно, предполагалось, что Когава приедет на такси. Имени и обратного адреса не было, только подпись — Море. Его приглашало море.

Когава не знал что делать. Если это не рекламный трюк, то кто и почему прислал приглашение? Возможно, кто-то из друзей решил подшутить над ним.

Садахико Когава все же принял приглашение — по трем причинам. Во-первых, он получил двадцать тысяч иен. Вернуть их он никак не мог. Если он не поедет — значит, взял деньги без должных оснований.

Второй — было естественное любопытство мужчины. Написала ему женщина. Она предлагала провести летнюю ночь в одном из лучших номеров нового отеля. Тут уж начинала работать фантазия...

Третьей причиной было любопытство журналиста. У человека, много лет проработавшего в еженедельном журнале, специализирующемся на индустрии развлечений, неизбежно развивается обостренное любопытство ко всему. А нос становится очень чувствительным.

Примерно месяц назад этот чувствительный нос повел его по следу, не имевшему никакого отношения к работе в журнале. Главный редактор потом строго отчитал его за это. Разразился скандал с известной певицей, и Когава поспешил на курорт Сирахама в префектуре Вакаяма. Певица скрывалась там после нашумевшей любовной истории. На курорте Когава с фотографом остановились в отеле «Боюсо», окнами выходившем на море. Певицу Когава найти никак не мог, она от всех пряталась. Однажды они засиделись у себя допоздна, разговаривали и не ложились спать. Часа в два ночи они услышали какой-то шум за окном. Их номер был на втором этаже. Фонари, которые не гасли в саду до утра, ярко освещали бетонную дорожку рядом с отелем. На бетоне лежала распластавшись молодая женщина, упав в западный стиль. Вокруг суетились охранники и служащие отеля.

Когава поспешил вниз. Он вышел через служебный вход и расспросил охранника, нашедшего тело, а также нескольких служащих. Женщину звали Судзуко Куме, ей было 25 лет. Жила она в № 515.

В этой комнате, в сумочке Судзуко, нашли три прощальные записки, которые обычно оставляют перед самоубийством: родителям, младшей сестре, которая путешествовала тогда в Европе, и администрации фирмы, где она работала. В записках Судзуко благодарила адресатов за все, что они для нее сделали, и извинялась за беспокойство, которое доставит им ее смерть. Она решила убить себя из-за безнадежной любовной связи с мужчиной, у которого были жена и дети. Экспертиза показала, что все три записки написаны рукой Судзуко.

Окно 515-й комнаты было открыто. Судя по всему, она выбросилась из этого окна.

Хотя родом Судзуко была из Канадзавы в префектуре Сиракава, жила она вместе с младшей сестрой в Токио. Сестра работала в бюро путешествий, которое посылало некоторых служащих гидами с туристическими группами. В одном из таких турне и была младшая сестра.

На телефонном коммутаторе отеля было отмечено, что непосредственно перед смертью Судзуко Куме целый час говорила по телефону с родителями в Канадзава. Это как-то не вязалось с

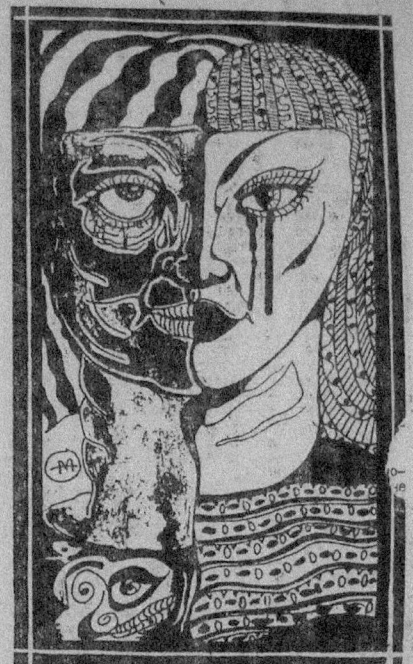

Get inspired

When you focus on success, you fall into the trap of comparing yourself to others, feeling envious. Instead, focus on getting better every day, focus on excellence. Gratitude floods your body and brain with emotions that uplift you and energize you. Use your strengths for a bigger purpose beyond yourself. Focus on what you are giving instead of what you are getting, it makes every your step more rewarding and meaningful.

Get black ink pen medium and piece of cardstock paper 8.5"x11".

You would like to create something very unique and that's not always easy to do. Learn how to connect to the Universe, open your mind to the higher powers.

Close your eyes for a moment. Imaging that your consciousness leaves your body and fly to the Space where there are no people there but only super speed and super powers. Forget about your daily life experiences with supermarkets and laundry stations. No noise should disturb you except, possible, music. You are not you any more, you are a part of the Universe.

Slowly open your eyes. Try not to look around, look only at your piece of plain white paper. This is the beginning. . . Now draw.

If you after all couldn't draw NeoPopRealism image, go to the next pages of this book. After you learn how to draw with the all offered tips and tricks, come back to this page again and let see what will happen.

How to create advanced realistic NeoPopRealist ink drawing

The following pages will show you how to create step-by-step advanced NeoPopRealism ink drawing "The Blind Royce". This is not an imaginative image of the car but a particular model of Rolls Royce, called D'Vinci. The background is imaginative. Every next drawing includes the new details. The final image looks like this:

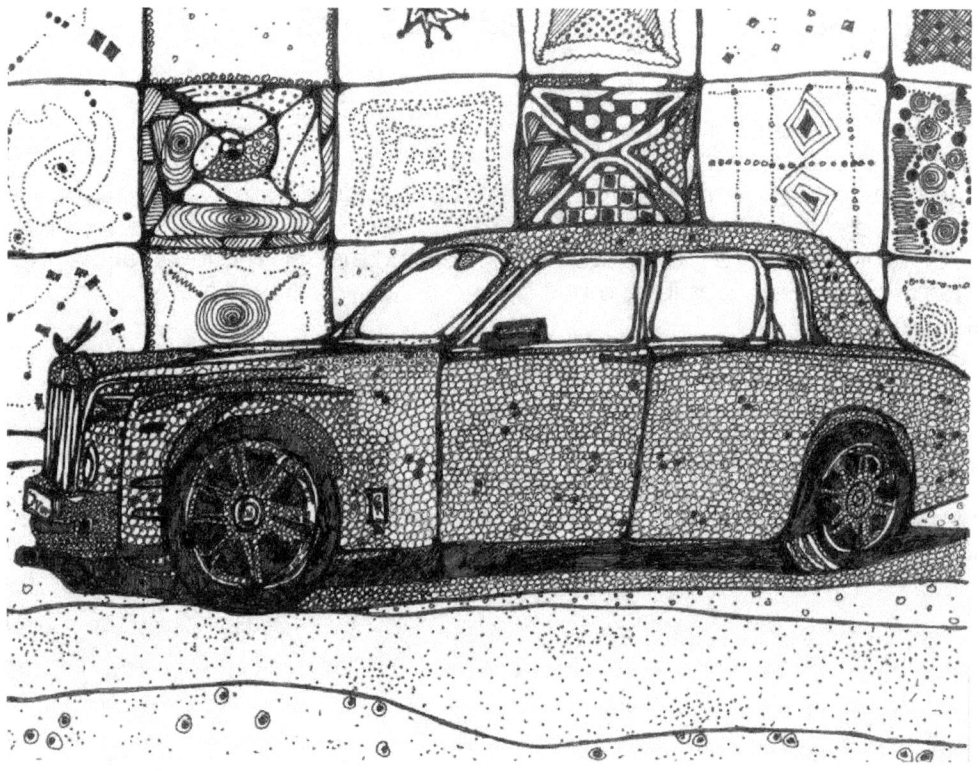

Nadia Russ, "The *Blind Royce*", ink on paper, 8.5"x11"

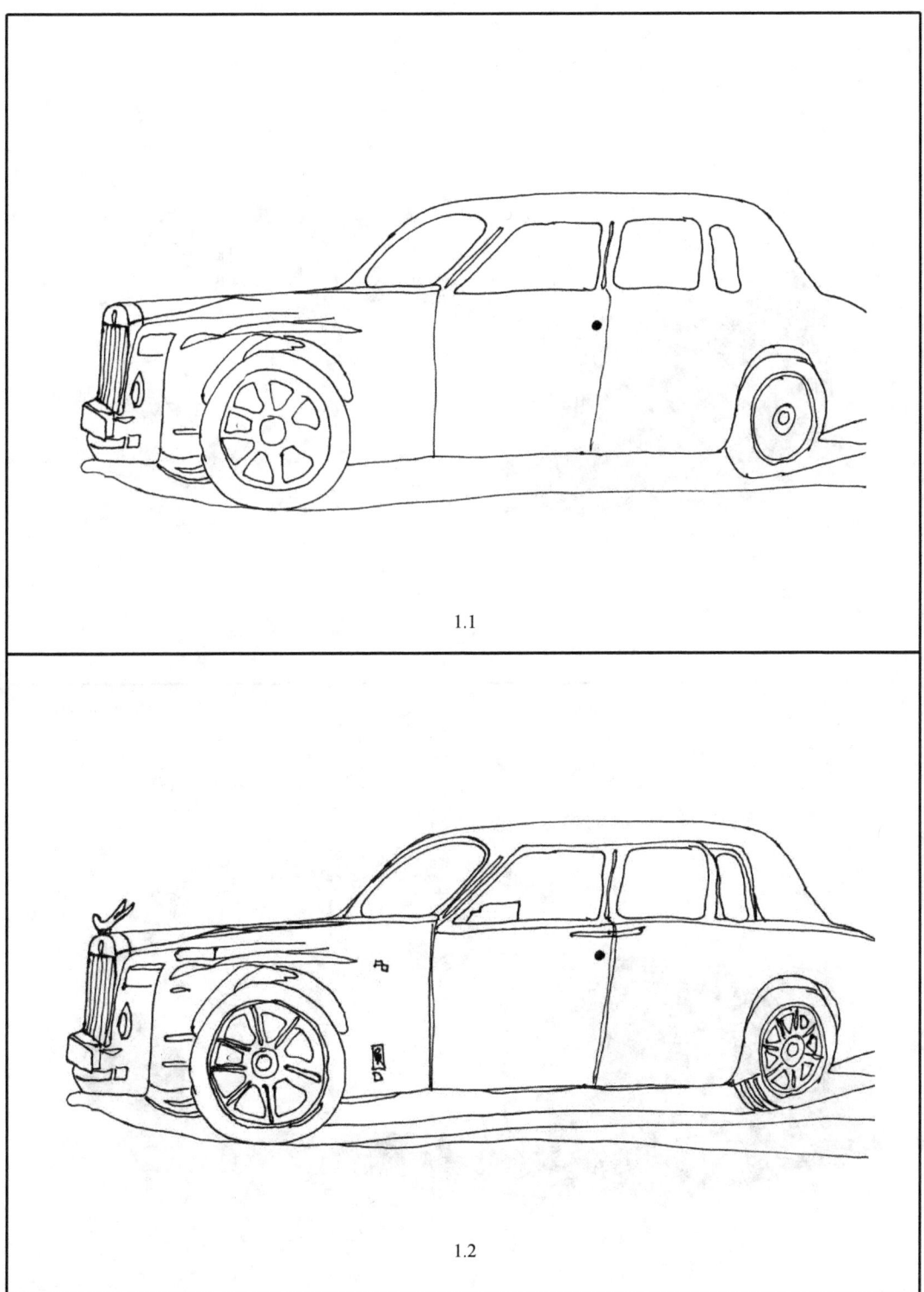

1.1

1.2

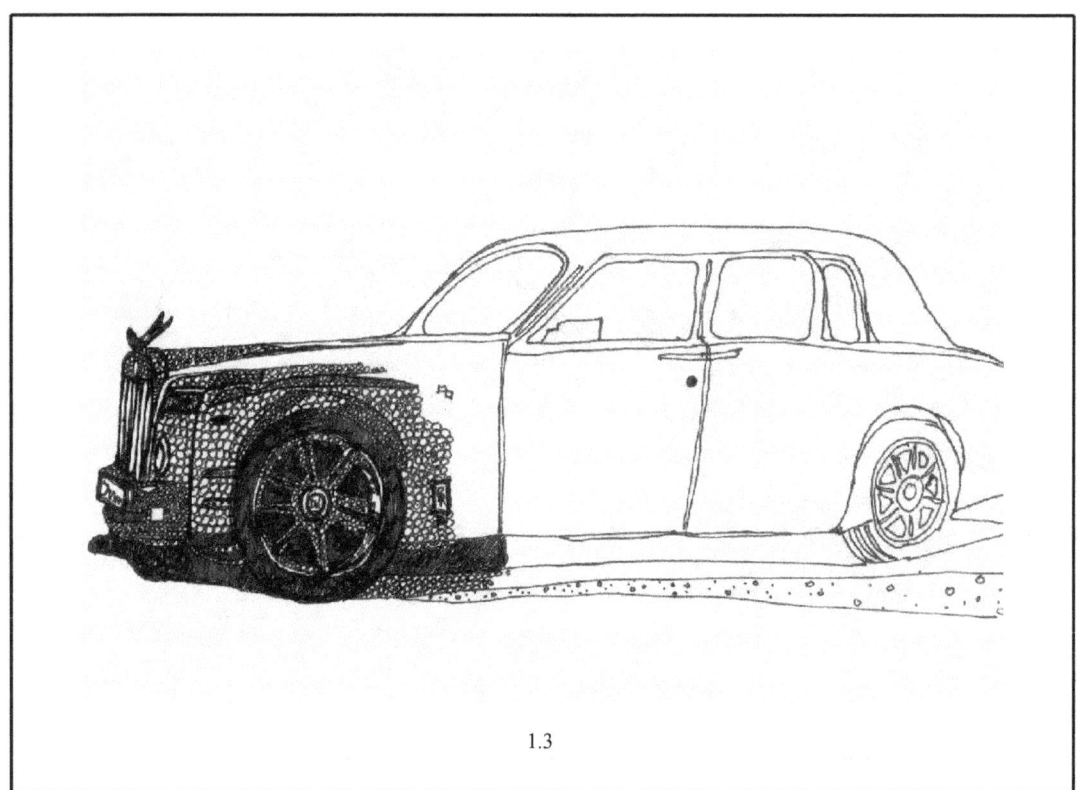

1.3

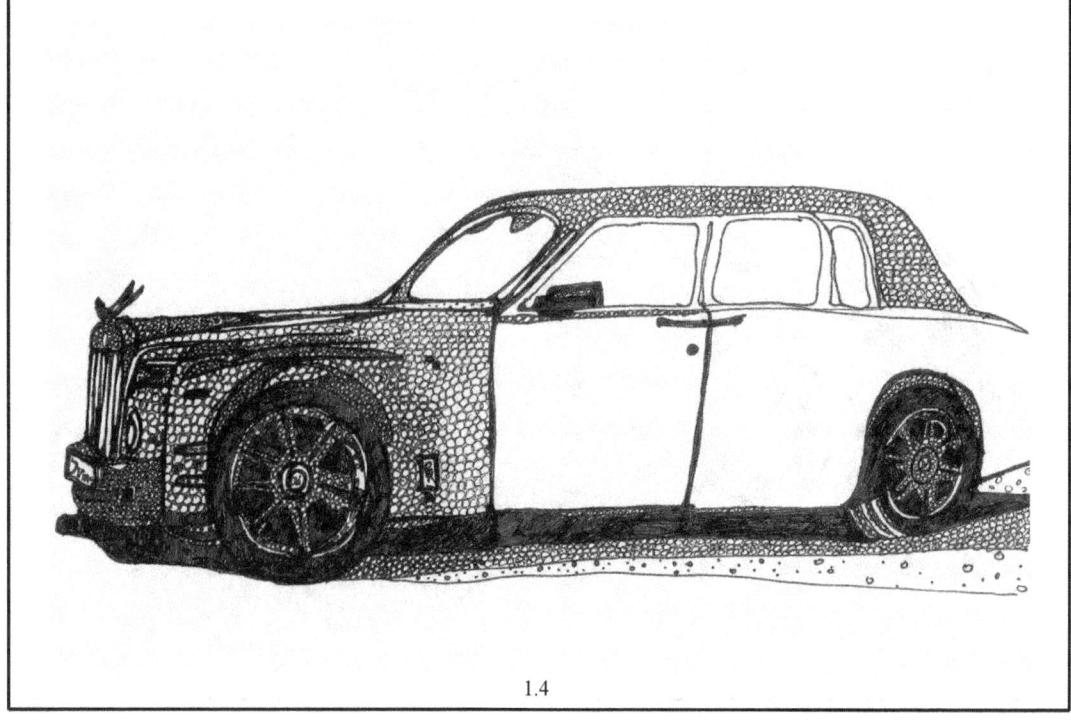

1.4

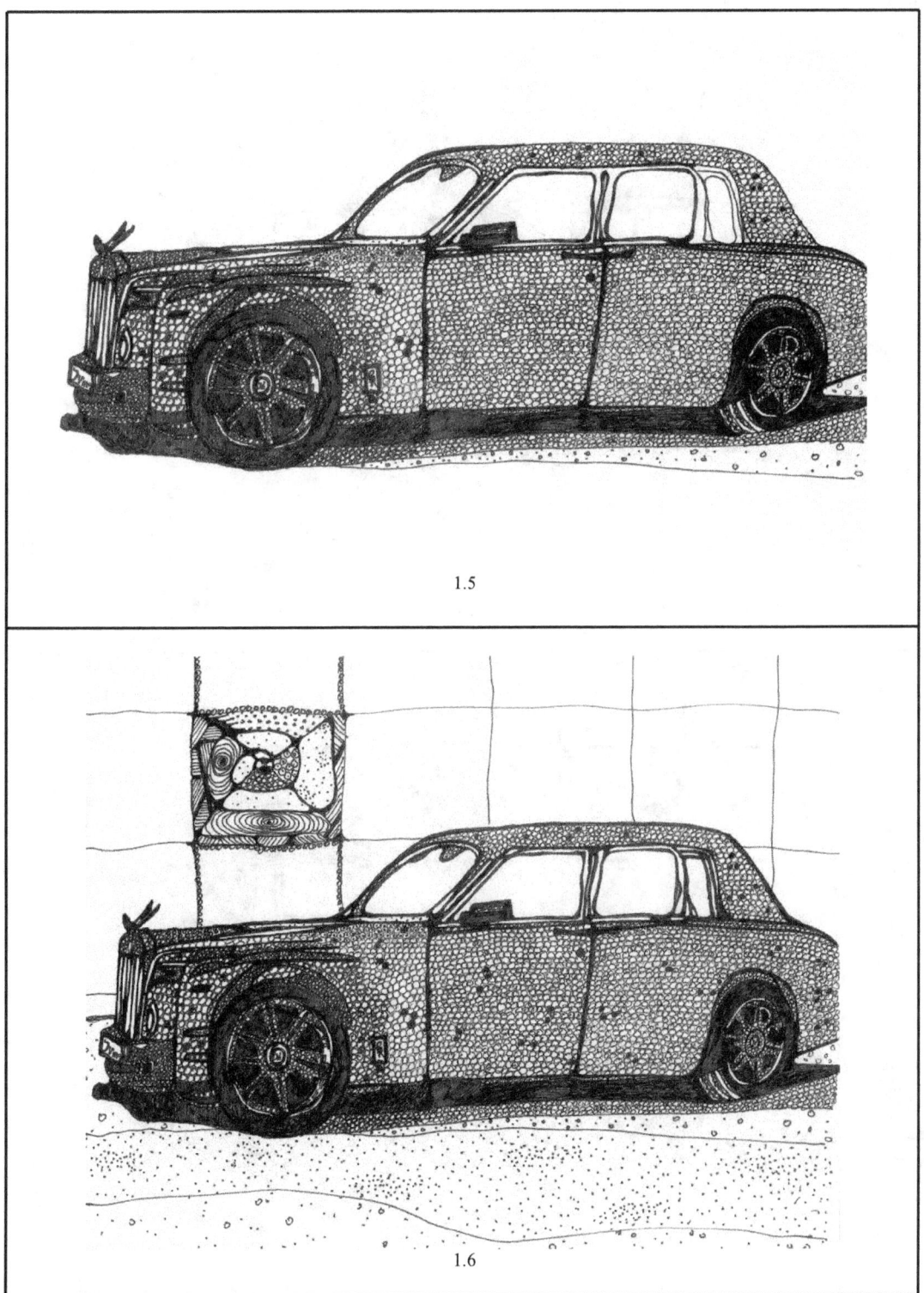

1.5

1.6

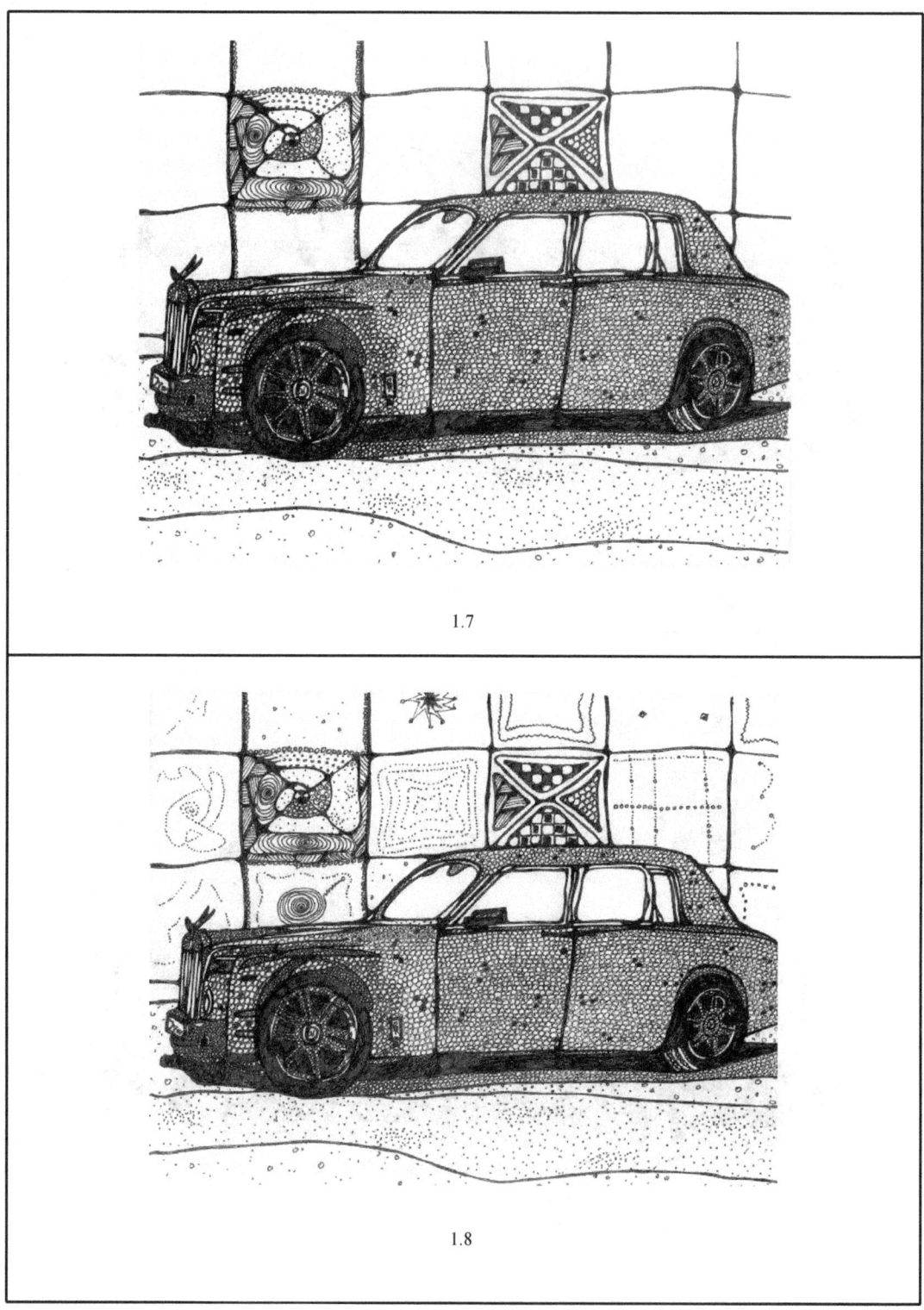

1.7

1.8

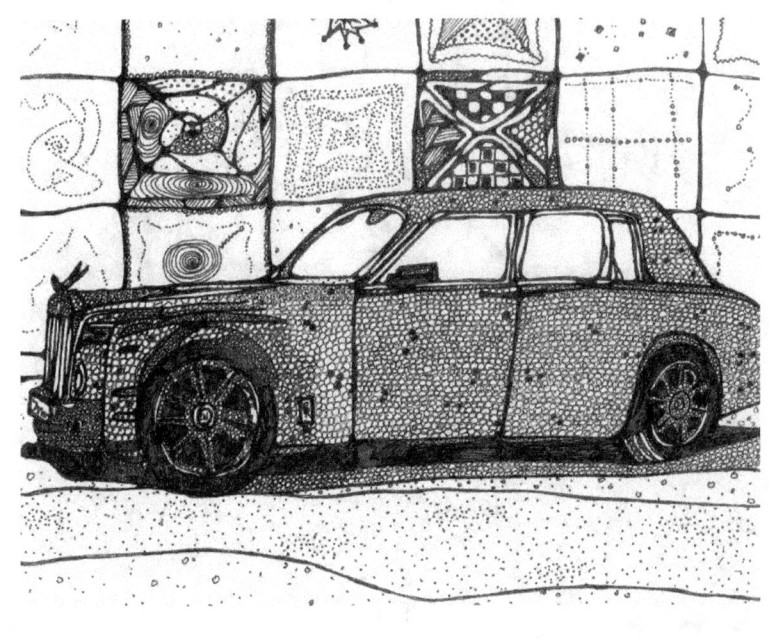

1.9

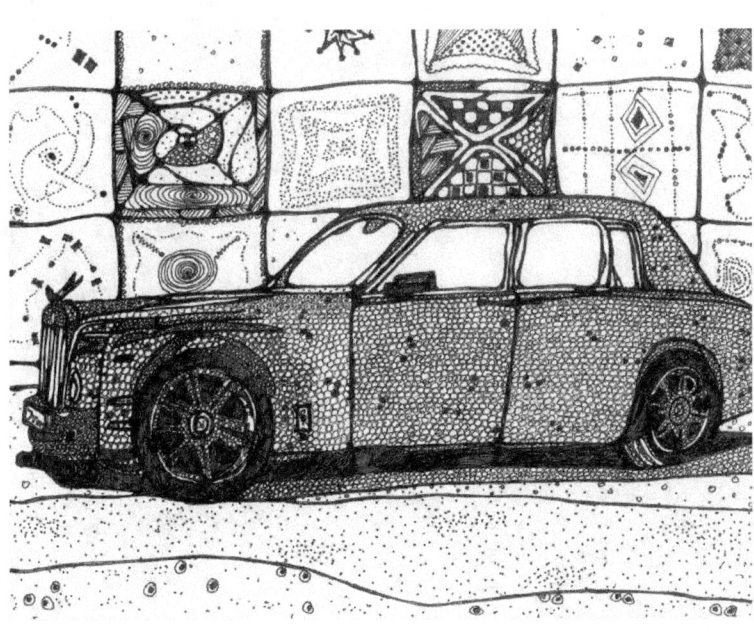

1.10

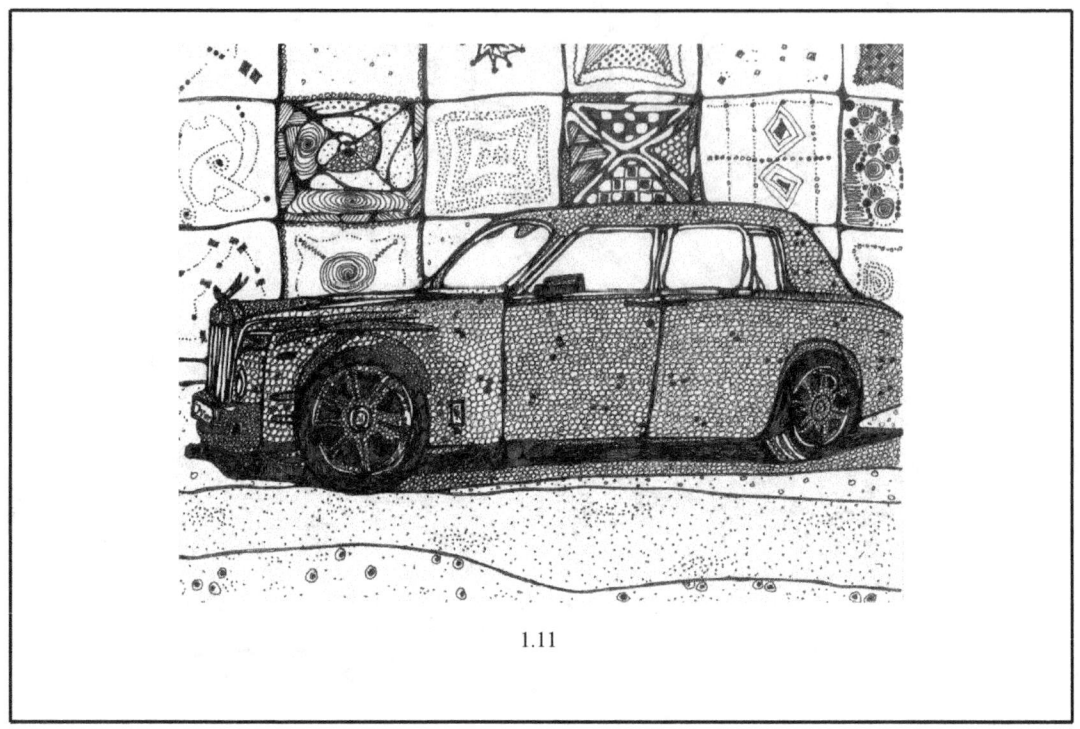

1.11

The following pages will show you how to draw some repetitive patterns and the background's design used in the advanced NeoPopRealism ink drawing "The *Blind Royce*." Every next image of each particular pattern includes the new detail(s). The drawing of the patterns is the meditative process, it helps to relax and increase brain's functionality as much, as develops your artistic skills.

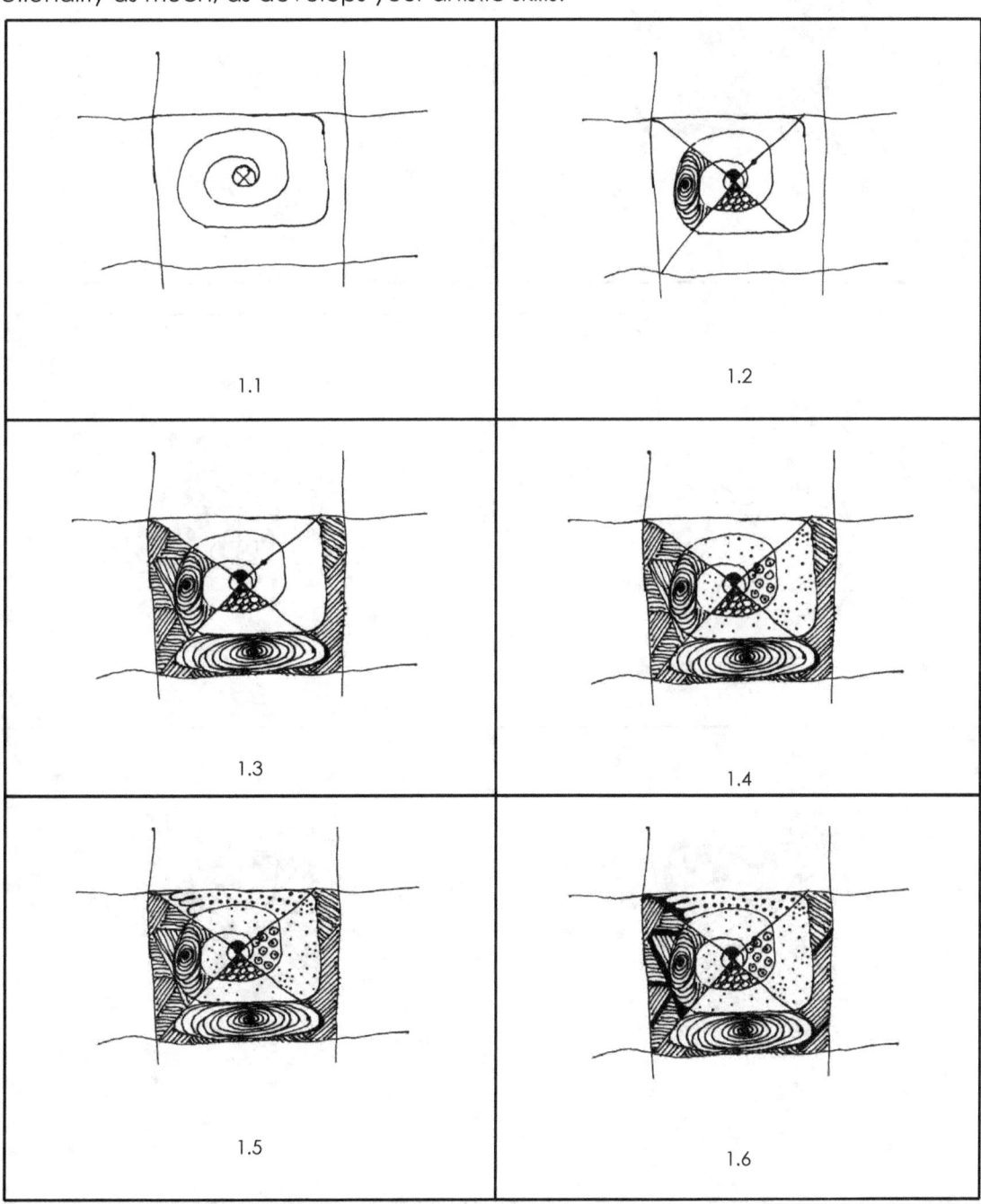

1.1

1.2

1.3

1.4

1.5

1.6

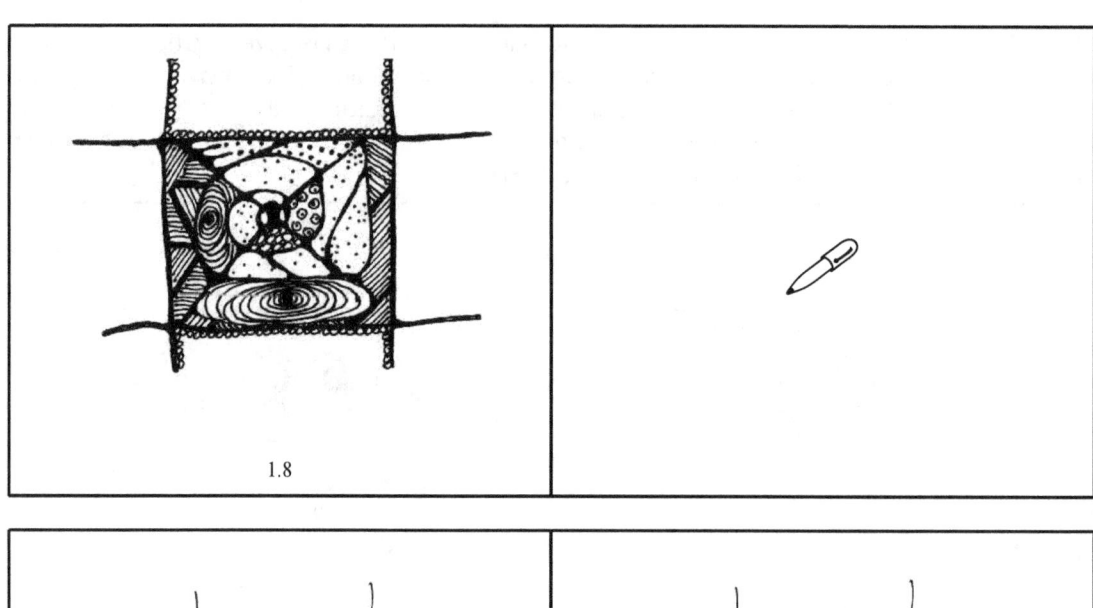

1.8

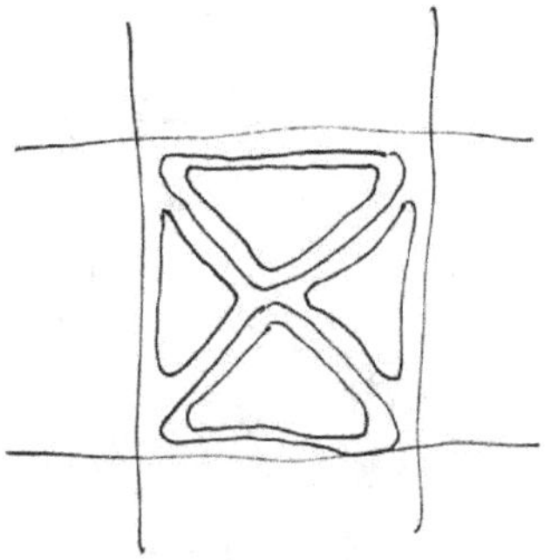

2.1

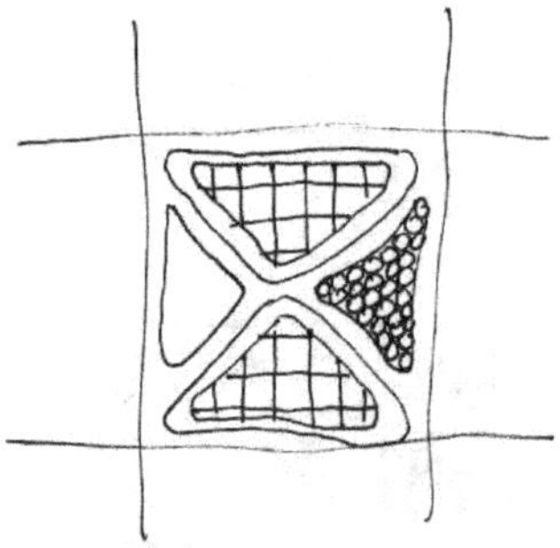

2.2

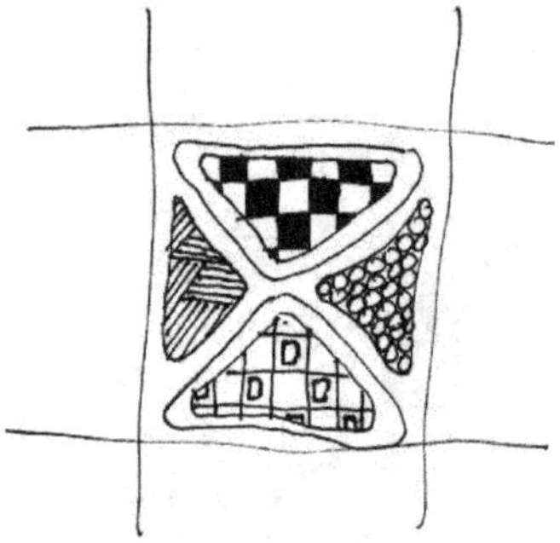

2.3

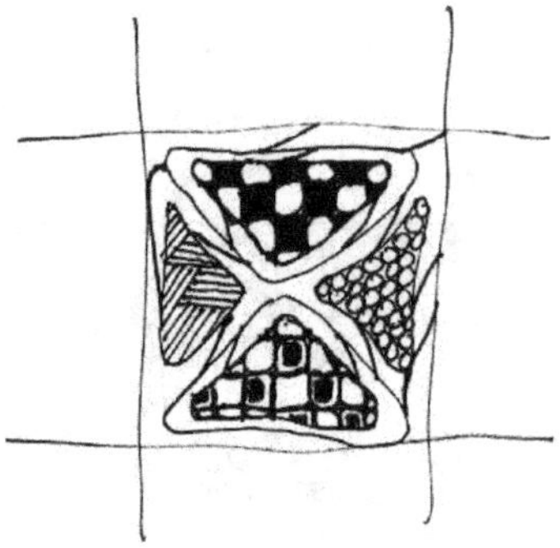

2.4

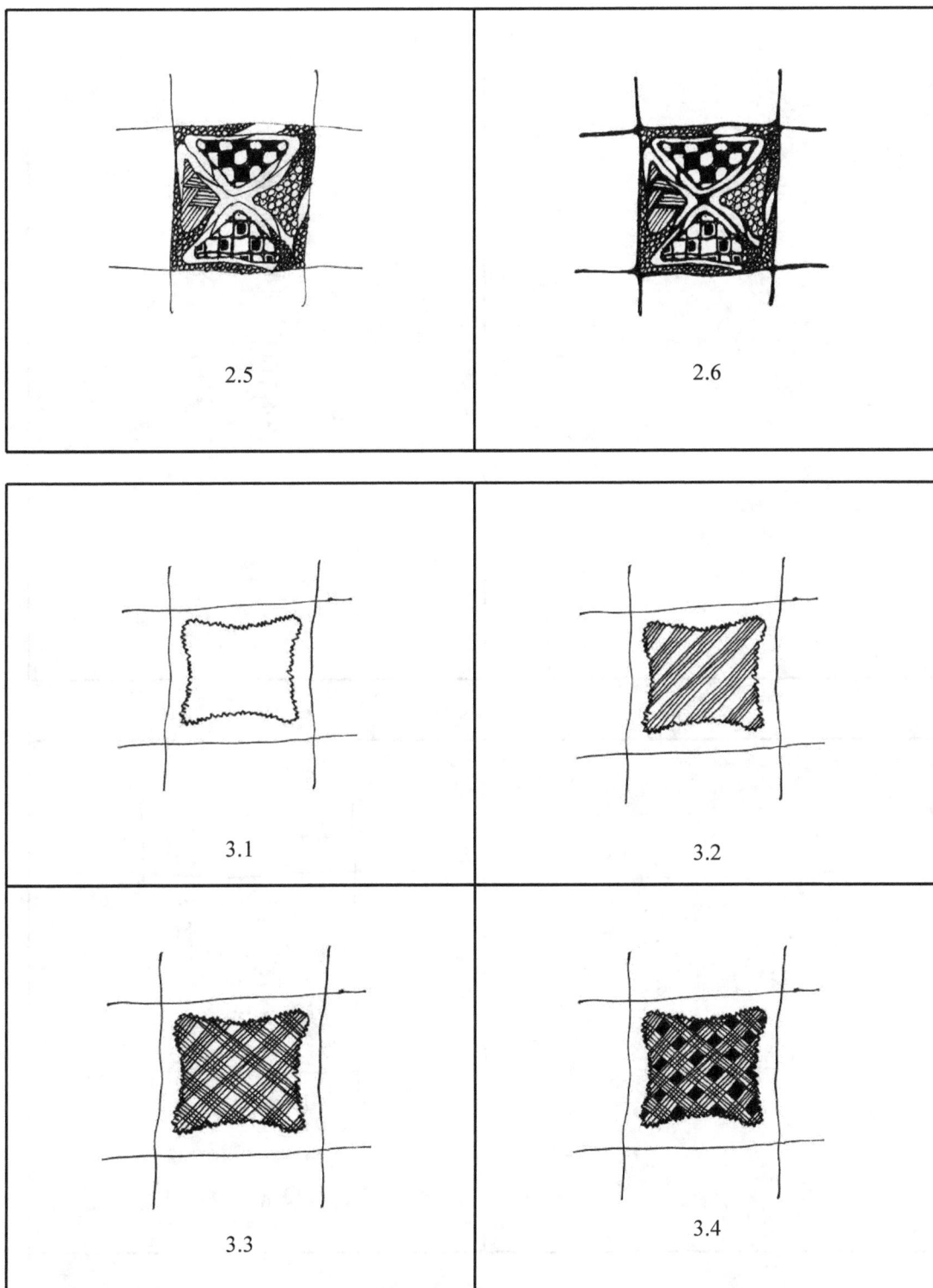

2.5

2.6

3.1

3.2

3.3

3.4

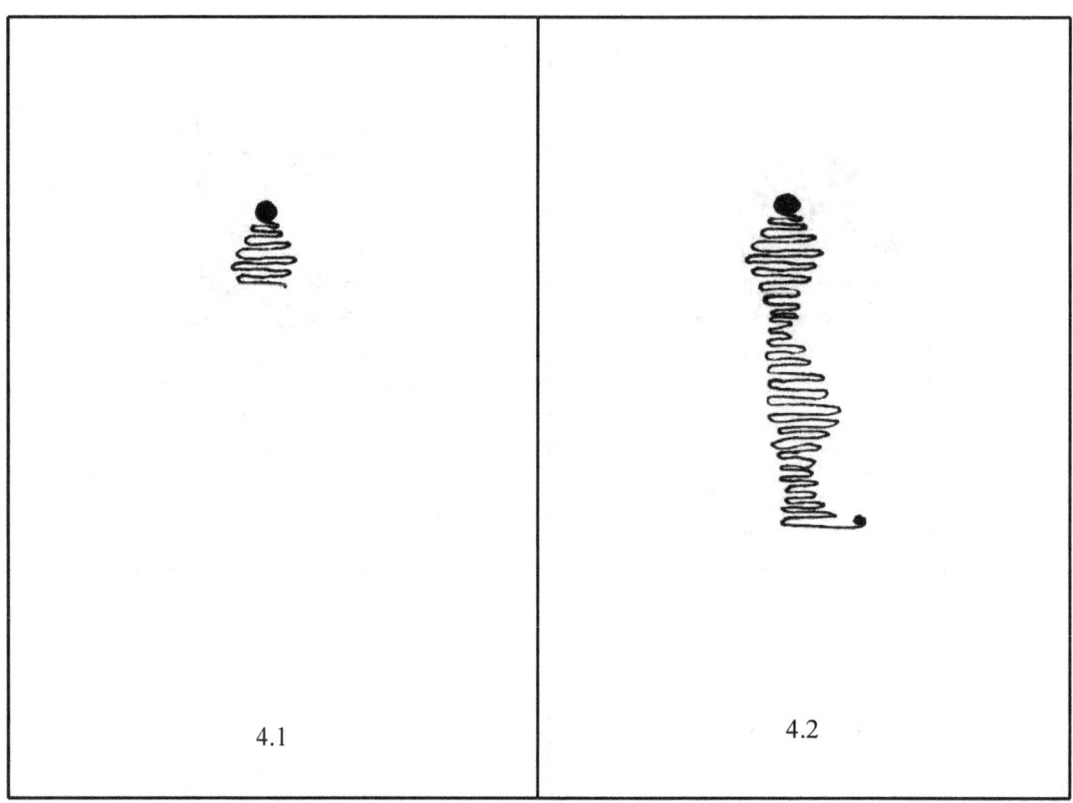

4.1

4.2

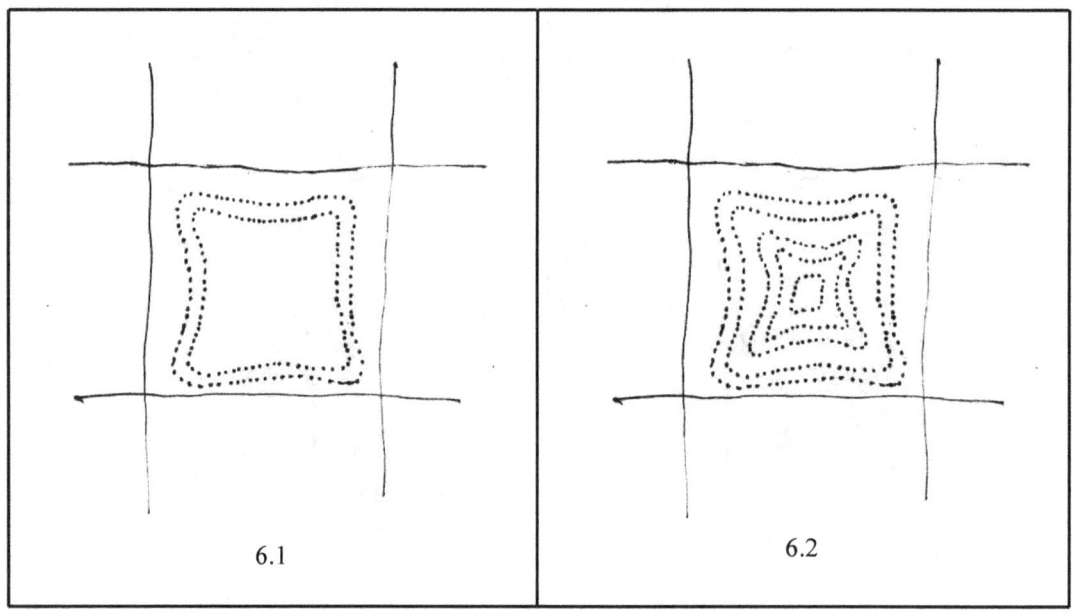

6.1

6.2

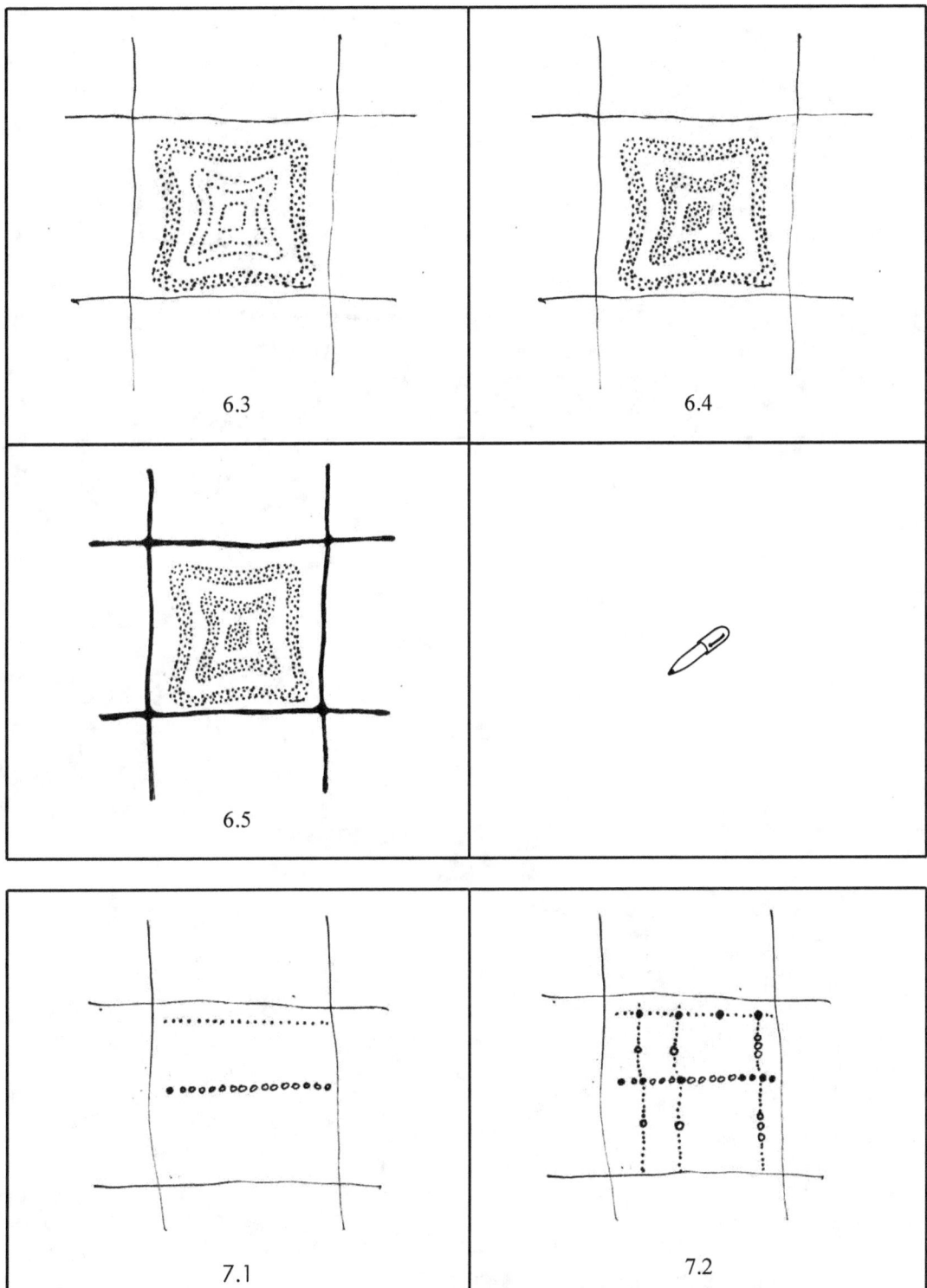

6.3

6.4

6.5

7.1

7.2

23

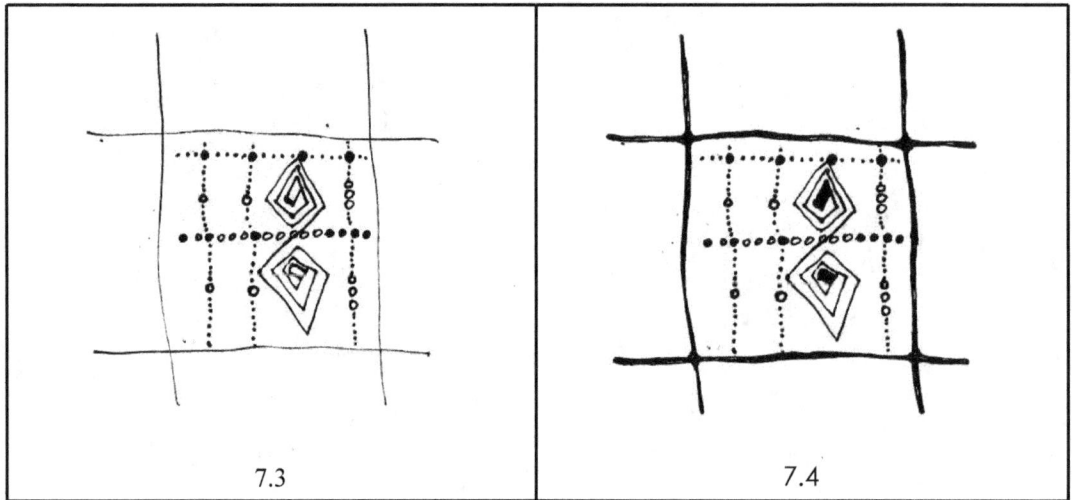

7.3   7.4

How to create imaginative NeoPopRealist ink drawings

The following pages will show you step-by-step how to create the imaginative advanced NeoPopRealism ink drawings. To create such drawings you need the artistic talent and particular skills. When you draw the imaginative images, you draw your mood, your feelings, yourself. This way of the self expression is related to your condition in a moment when you draw the image. The drawing these images is like the playing the music's compositions of Bach (German composer) or the American jazz, it depends on a subject of your drawing and your mood. The lines are like the melodies, which move seemed unpredictably, creating the harmonious compositions.

In a following drawing the line is flowing freely. You fill the appeared sections with the repetitive patterns. Every next image includes the new additional details. This is how a final drawing looks:

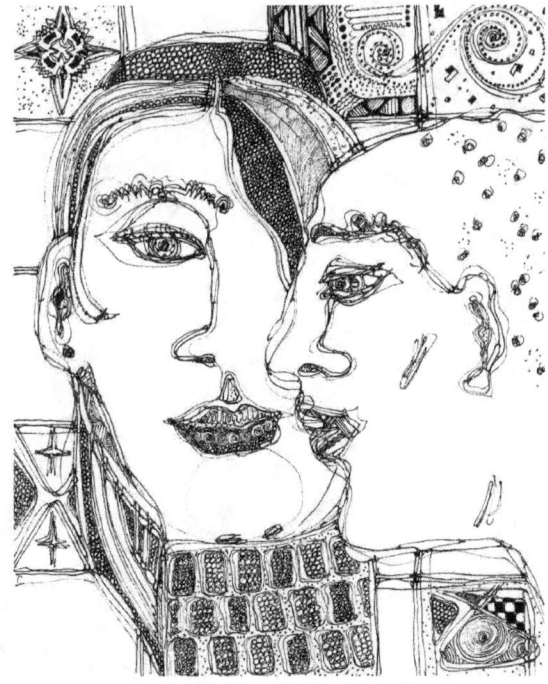

Nadia Russ, *Two Faces*, ink on paper, 8.5"x11"

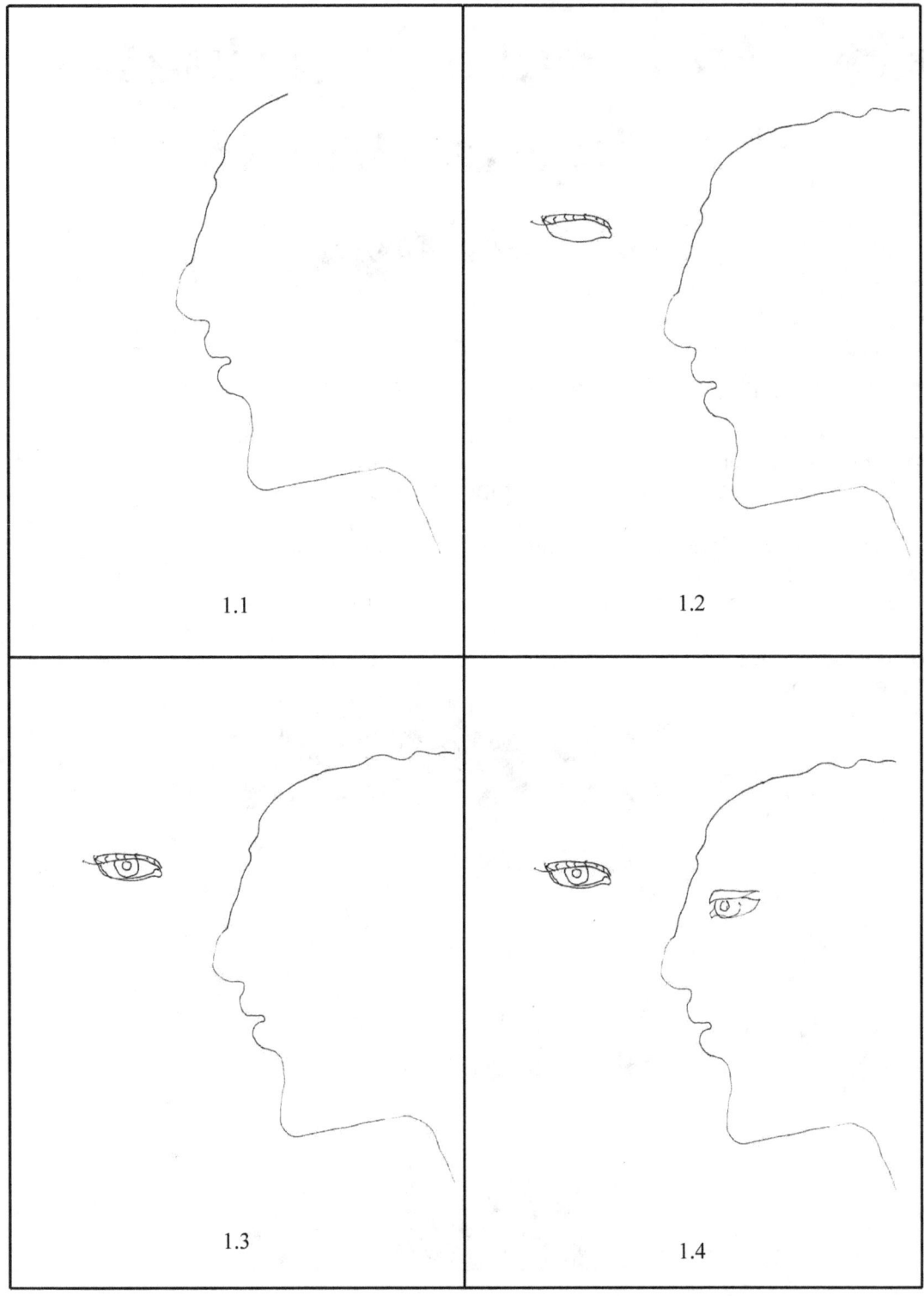

1.1

1.2

1.3

1.4

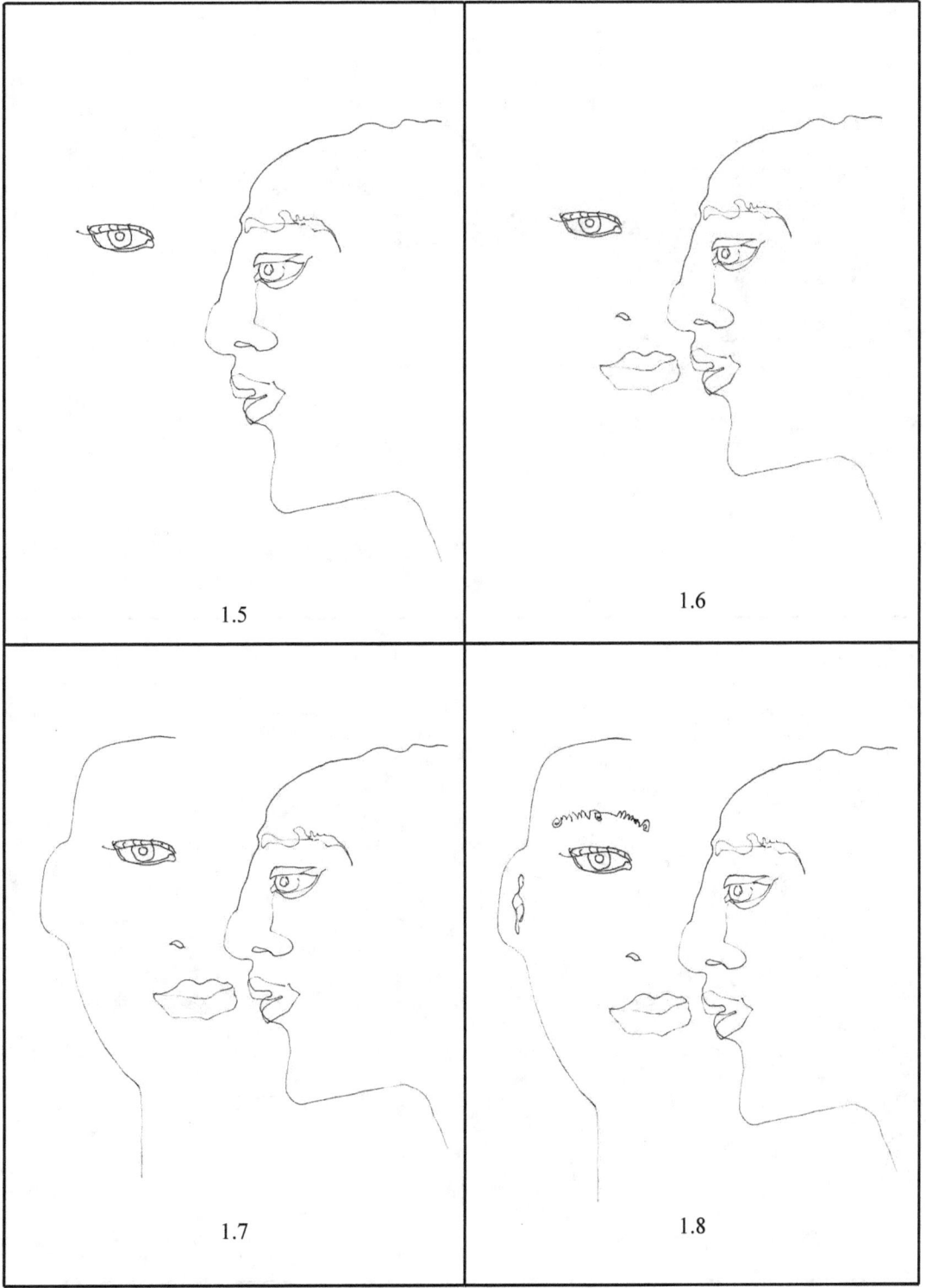

1.5

1.6

1.7

1.8

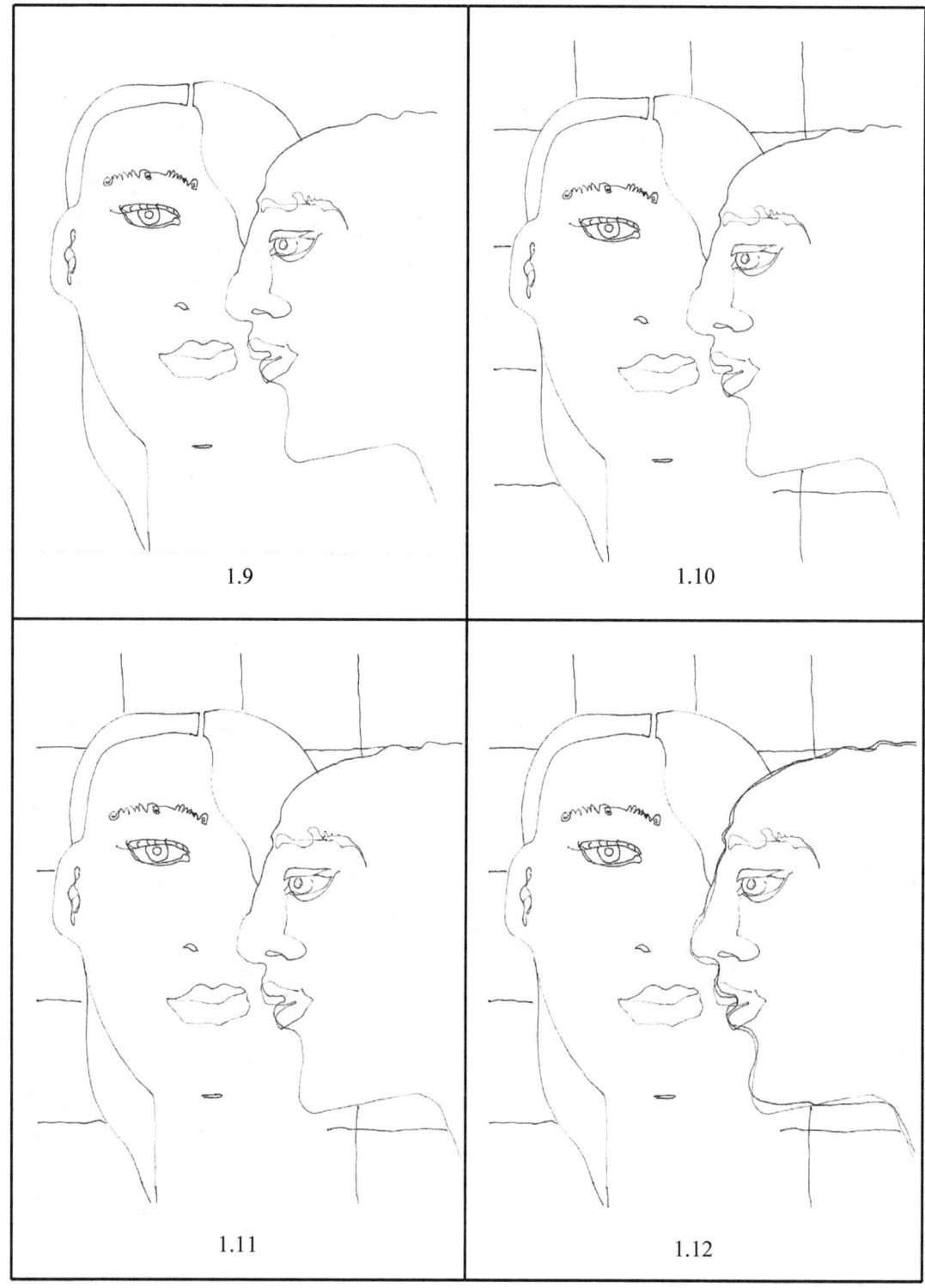

1.9

1.10

1.11

1.12

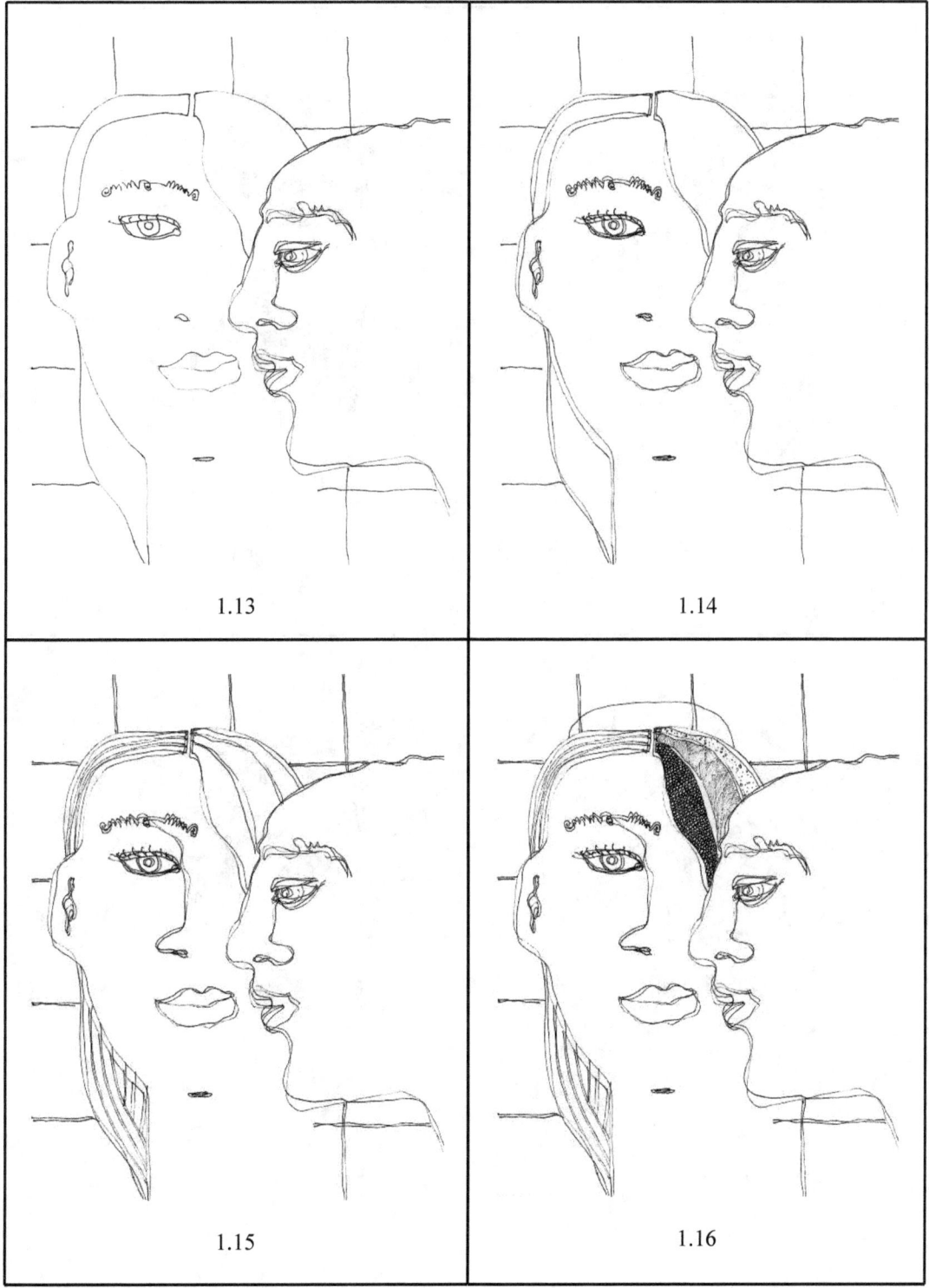

1.13

1.14

1.15

1.16

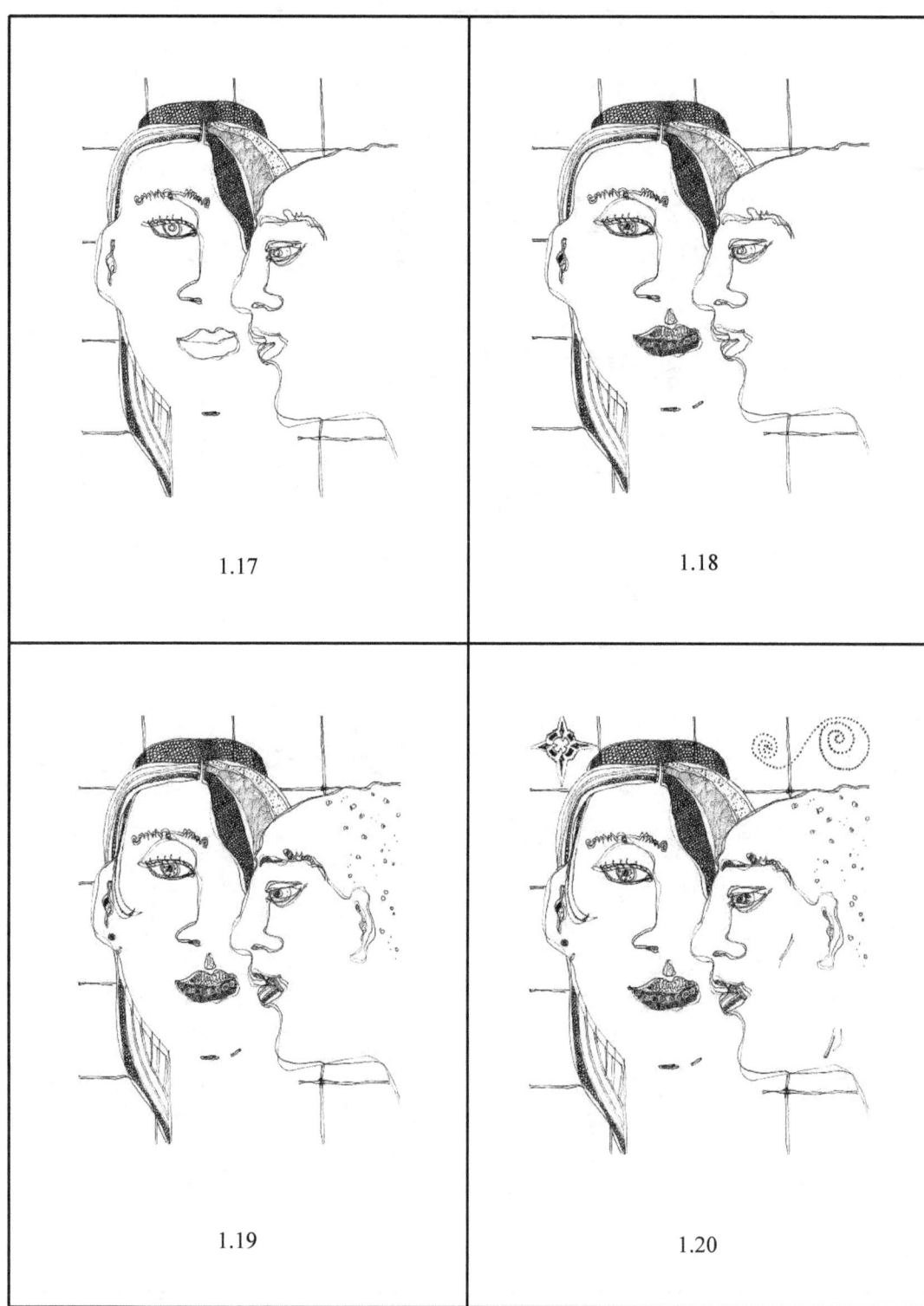

1.17

1.18

1.19

1.20

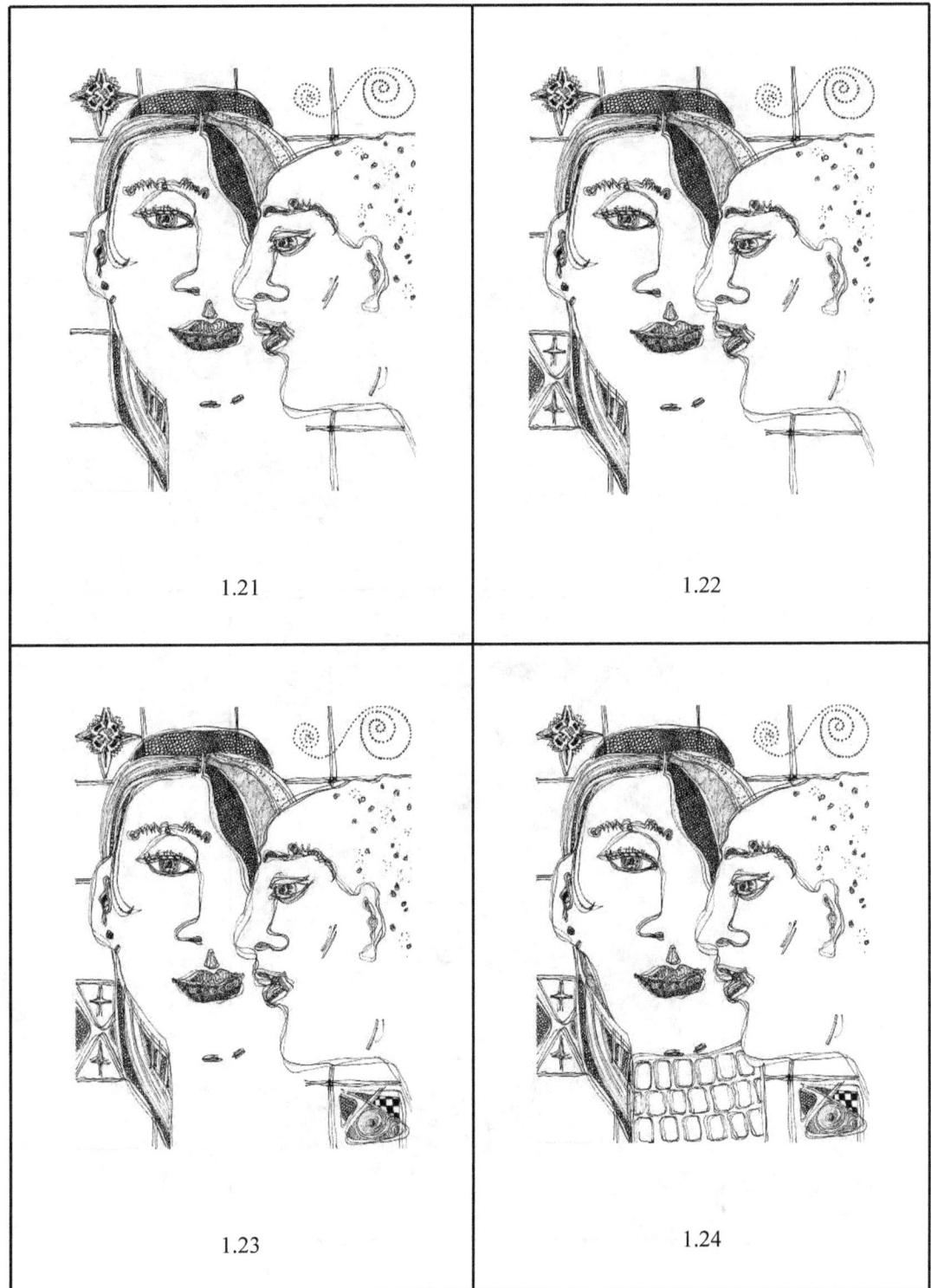

1.21

1.22

1.23

1.24

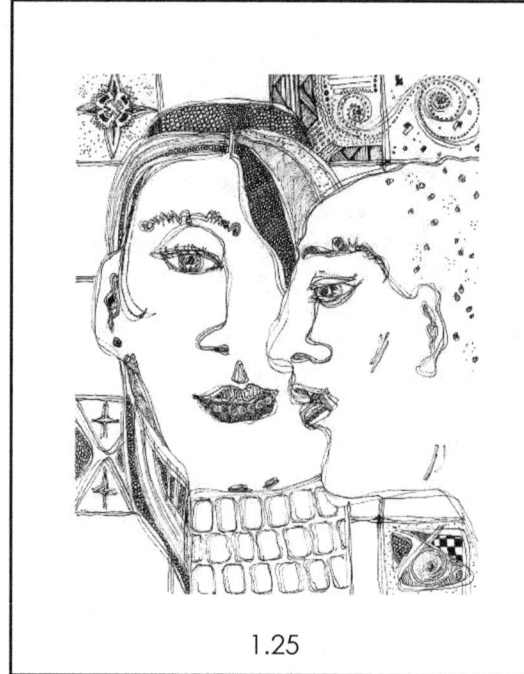

1.25

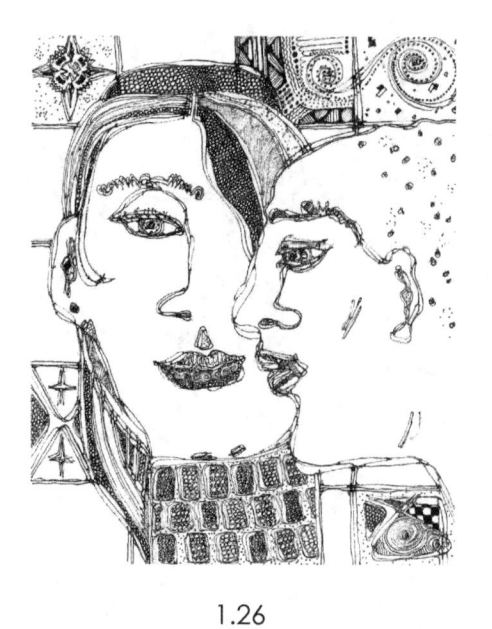

1.26

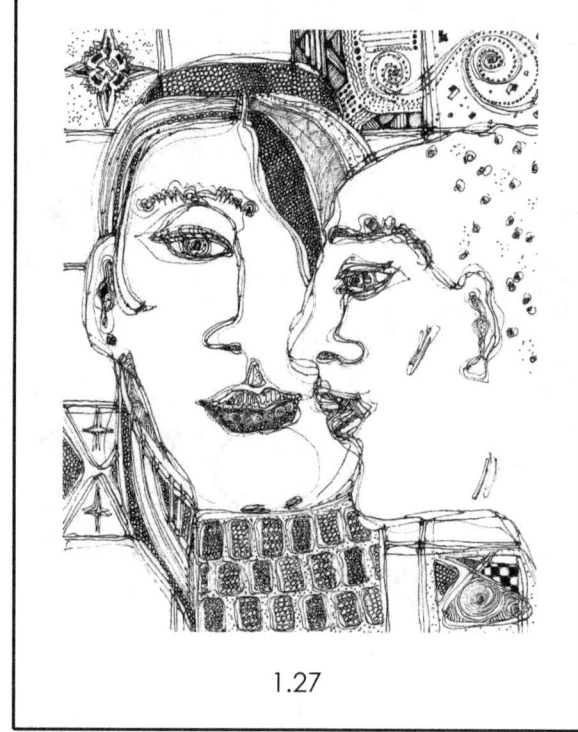

1.27

The following pages show you step-by-step how to create some designs and repetitive patterns used in a drawing *"Two Faces."* The repetitive patterns' drawing helps you to experience calm, ease, and peace of mind. It increases your energy and vitality and regulates your natural healing hormones. Why? Because when we draw the repetitive patterns, we enter the meditative state of mind, the highest state in which our brain can exist.

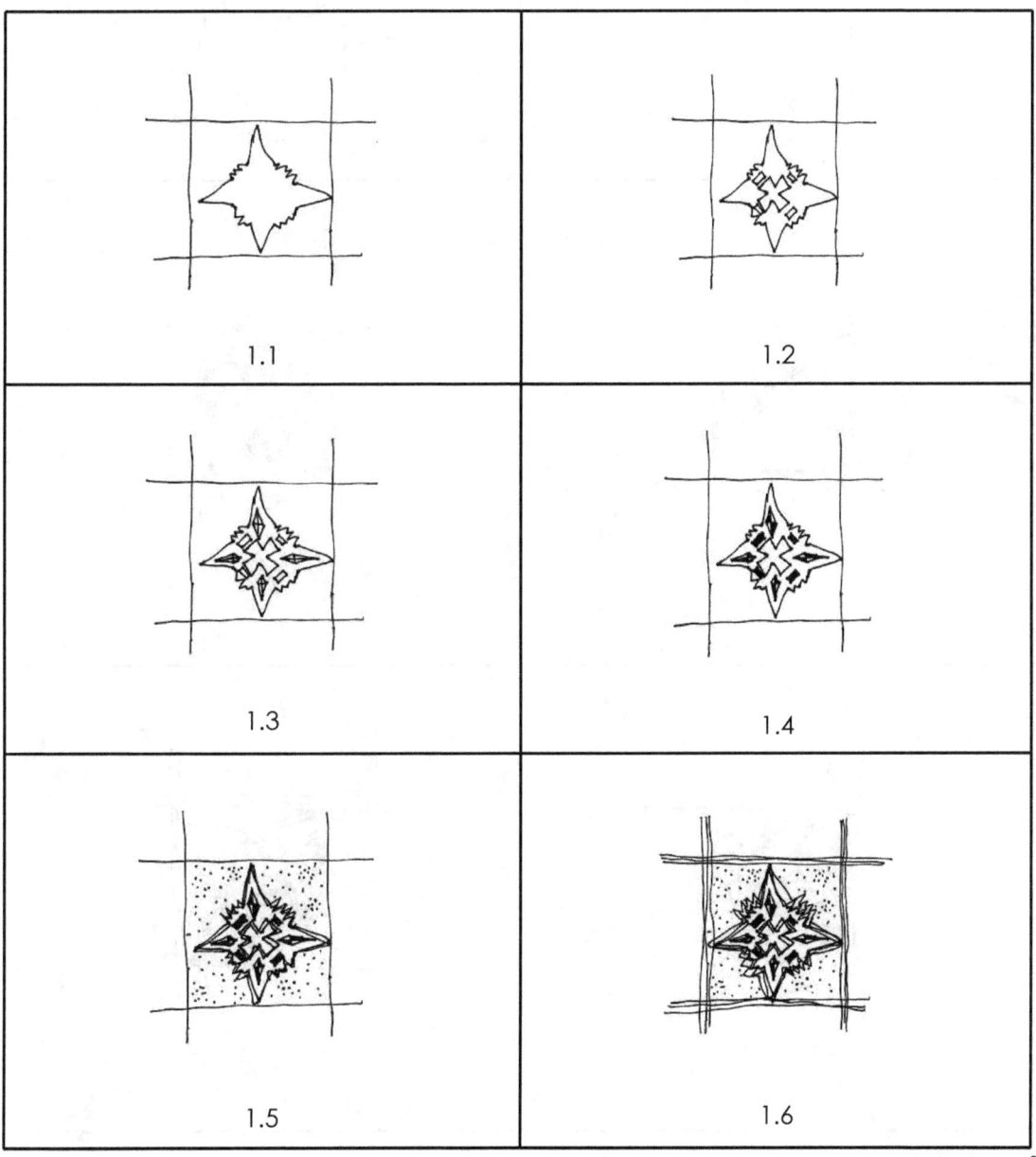

1.1

1.2

1.3

1.4

1.5

1.6

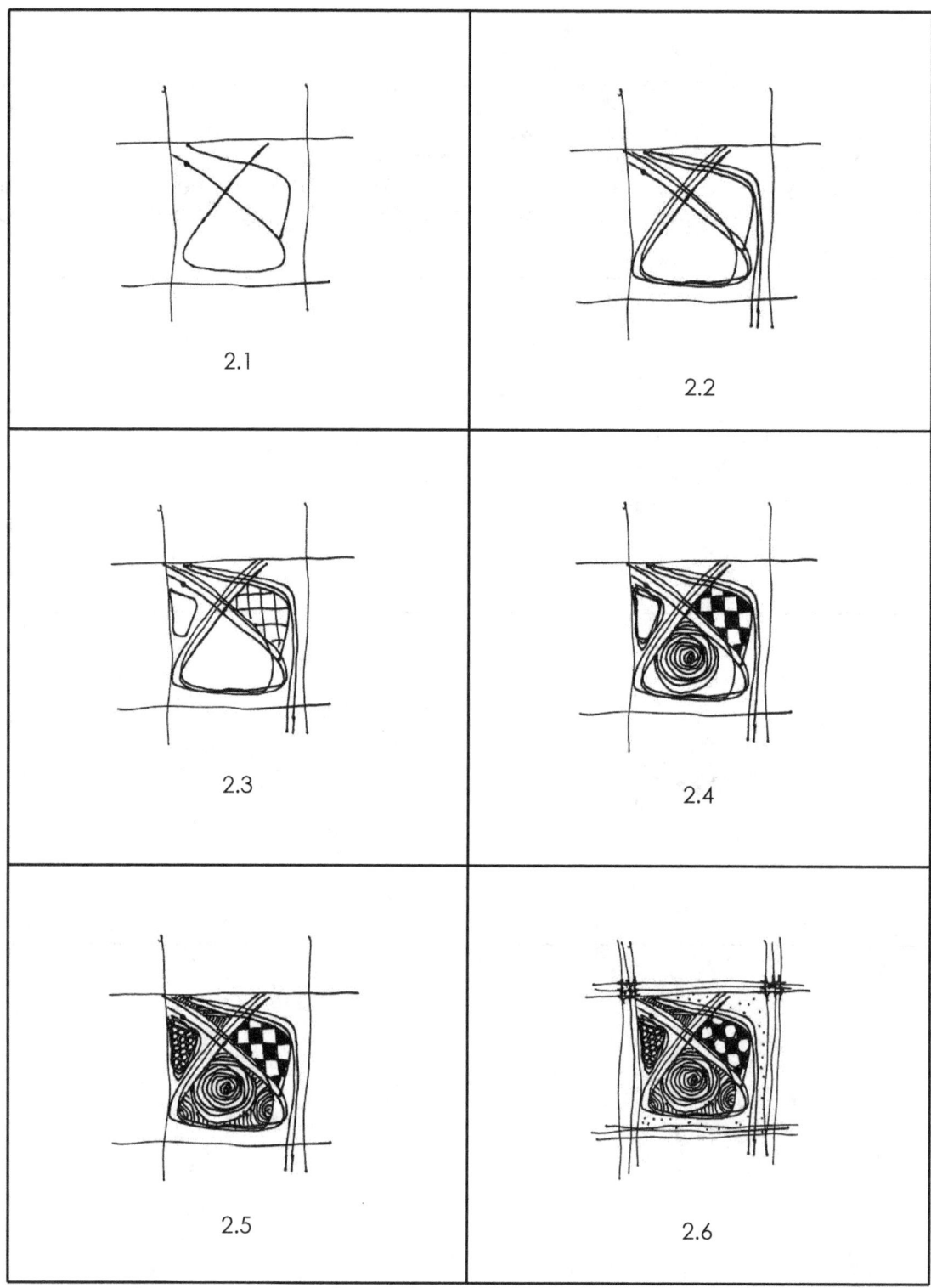

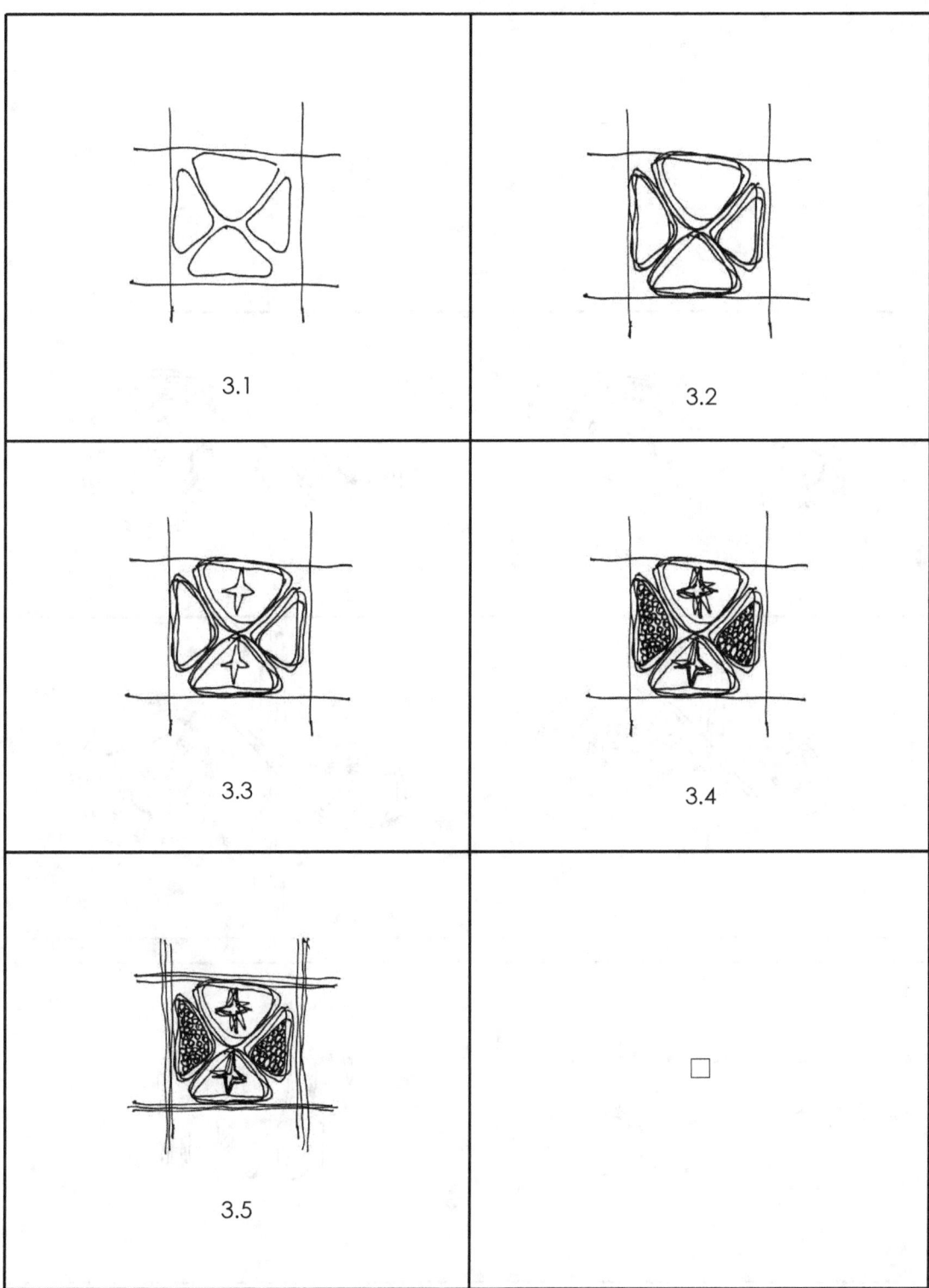

3.1

3.2

3.3

3.4

3.5

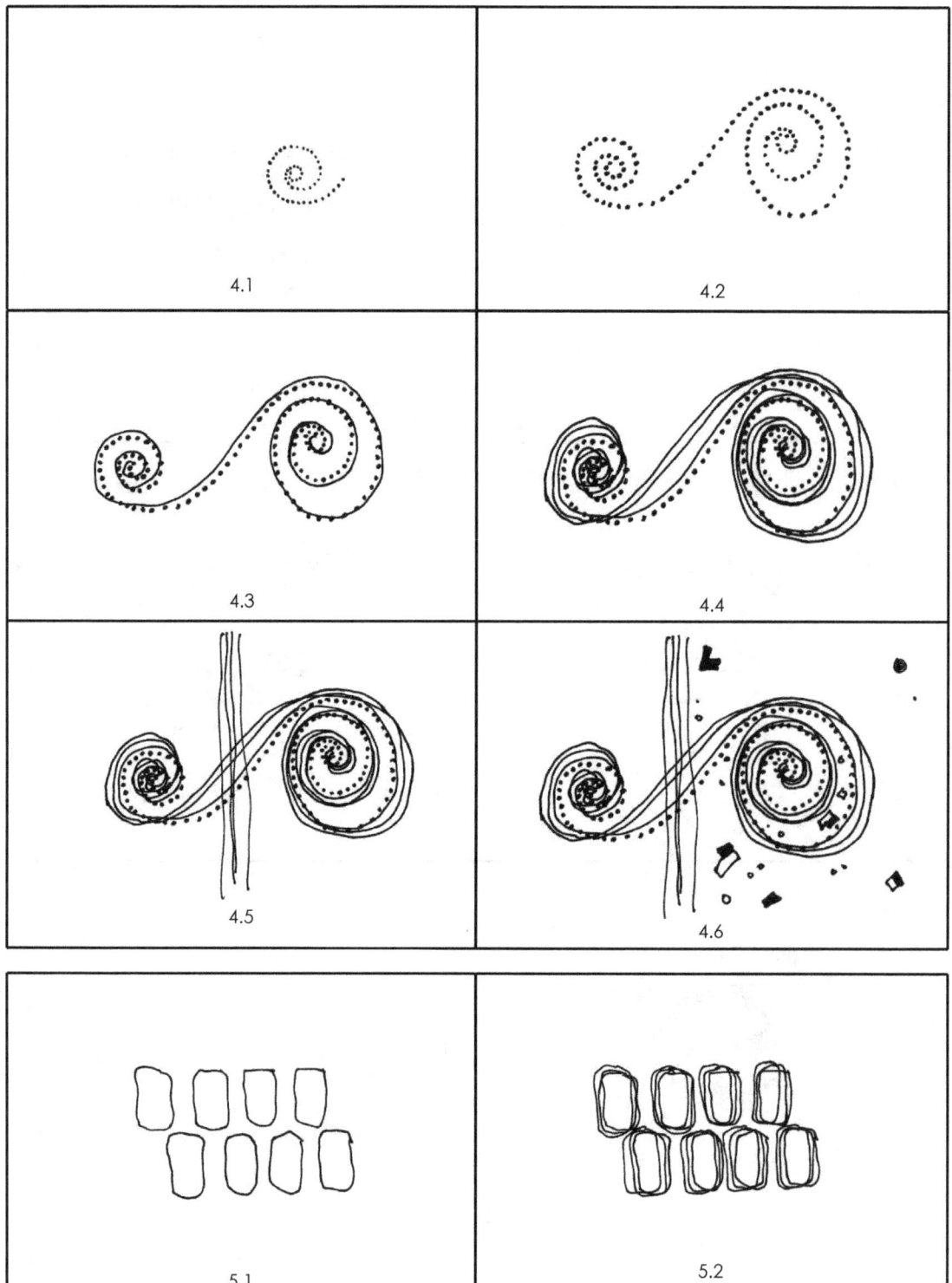

4.1

4.2

4.3

4.4

4.5

4.6

5.1

5.2

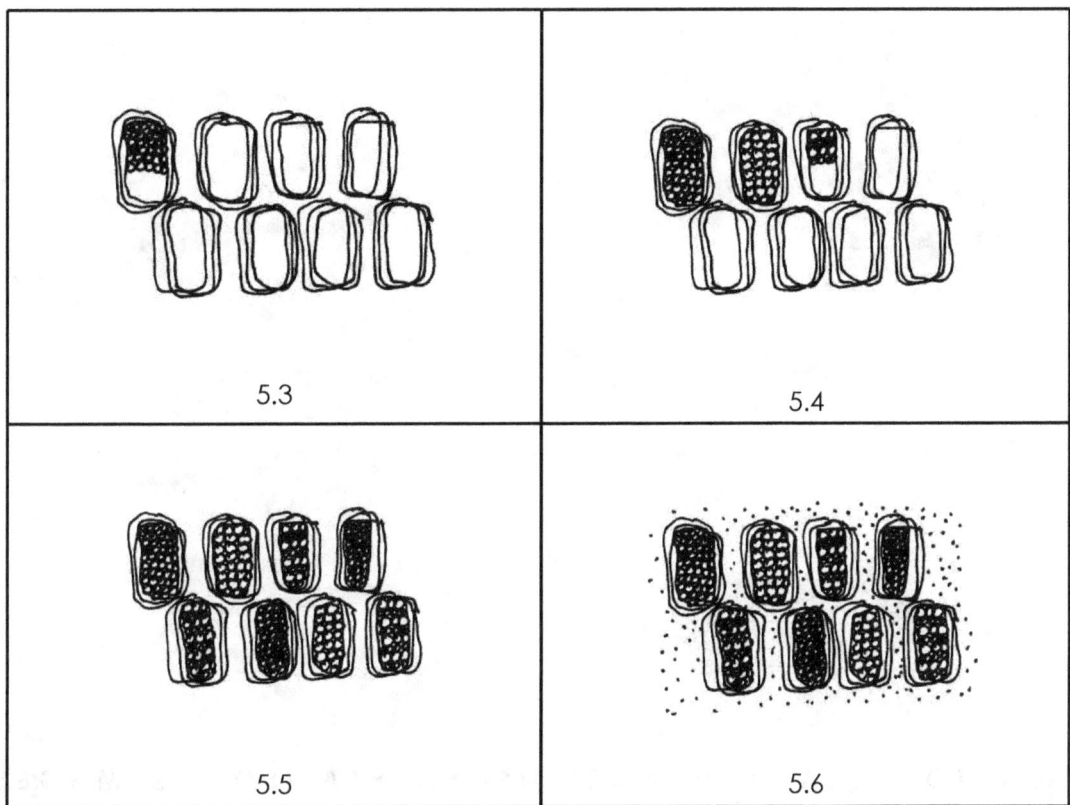

5.3

5.4

5.5

5.6

HOW TO DRAW ADVANCED NEOPOPREALISM INK IMAGES

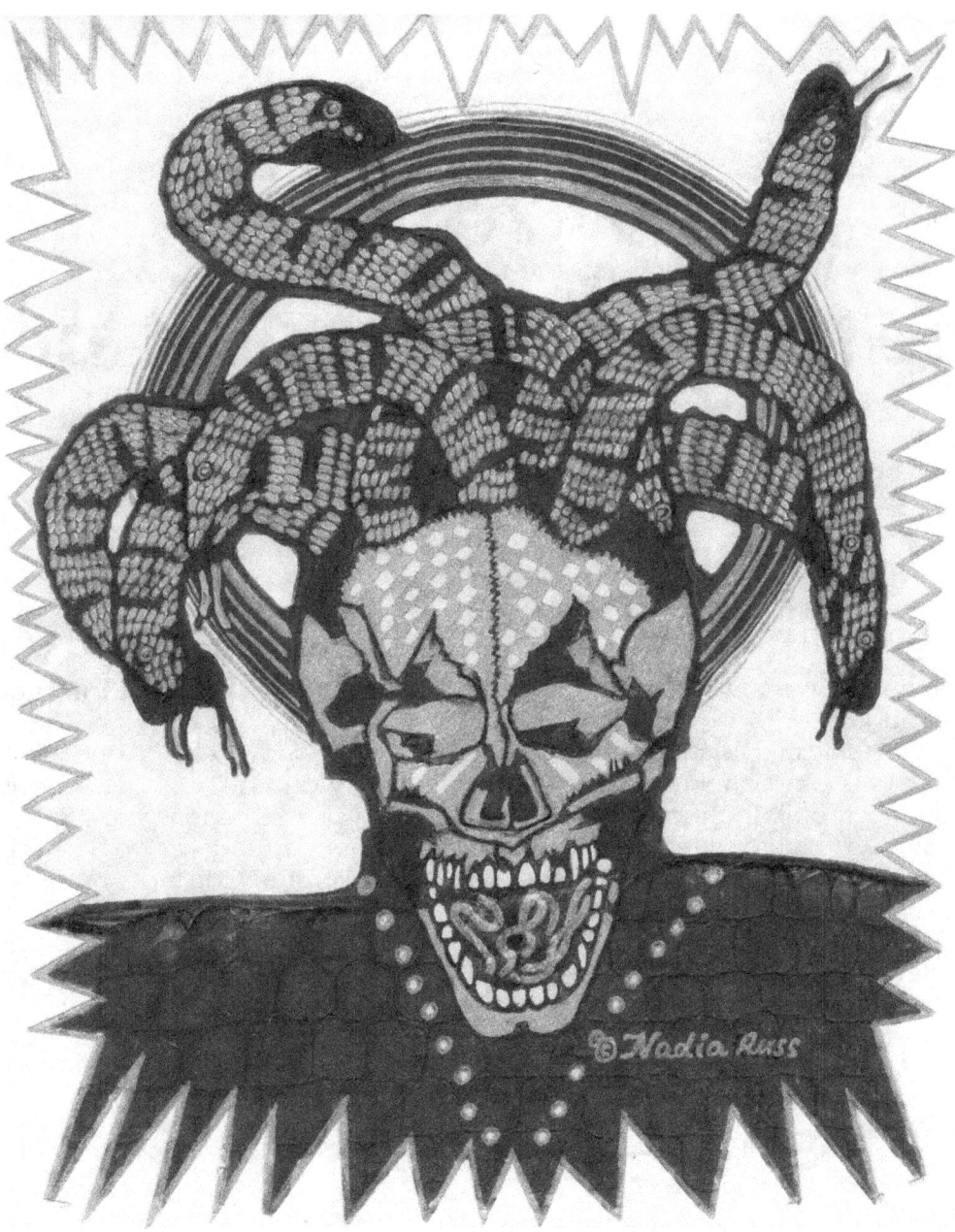

Nadia Russ, "*Skull*", black and silver ink pen on paper, 5"x8,5", 2004

Draw repetitive patterns here and now

The following pages invite you to complete the offered images. Draw here and now.

All you need is the thin ink pen because the thick ink pen will leave the marks on another side of pages.

Our world is fast and challenging, fun and demanding, exciting and frightening. It produces the emotional reactions; often stress, worry and anxiety, but we can tolerate only so much of it. The repetitive patterns' drawing process opens you the doors to the level of meditation and relaxation you never experienced before. Practice the drawing daily and you will be able to discover new you, with the wide eyes open to the new opportunities in arts and life in general.

Complete the following drawings using the flowing line and repetitive patters. The drawing repetitive patterns is intuitive process. Use your imagination, follow your creative instinct - the piece of paper is your playground. Probably, you have recognized in next image Amy Winehouse, the English singer-song-writer who was famous for her deep contralto. On 14 February 2007, she won a BRIT Award for the Best British Female Artist. Amy Winehouse died July 23, 2011 at age of 28.

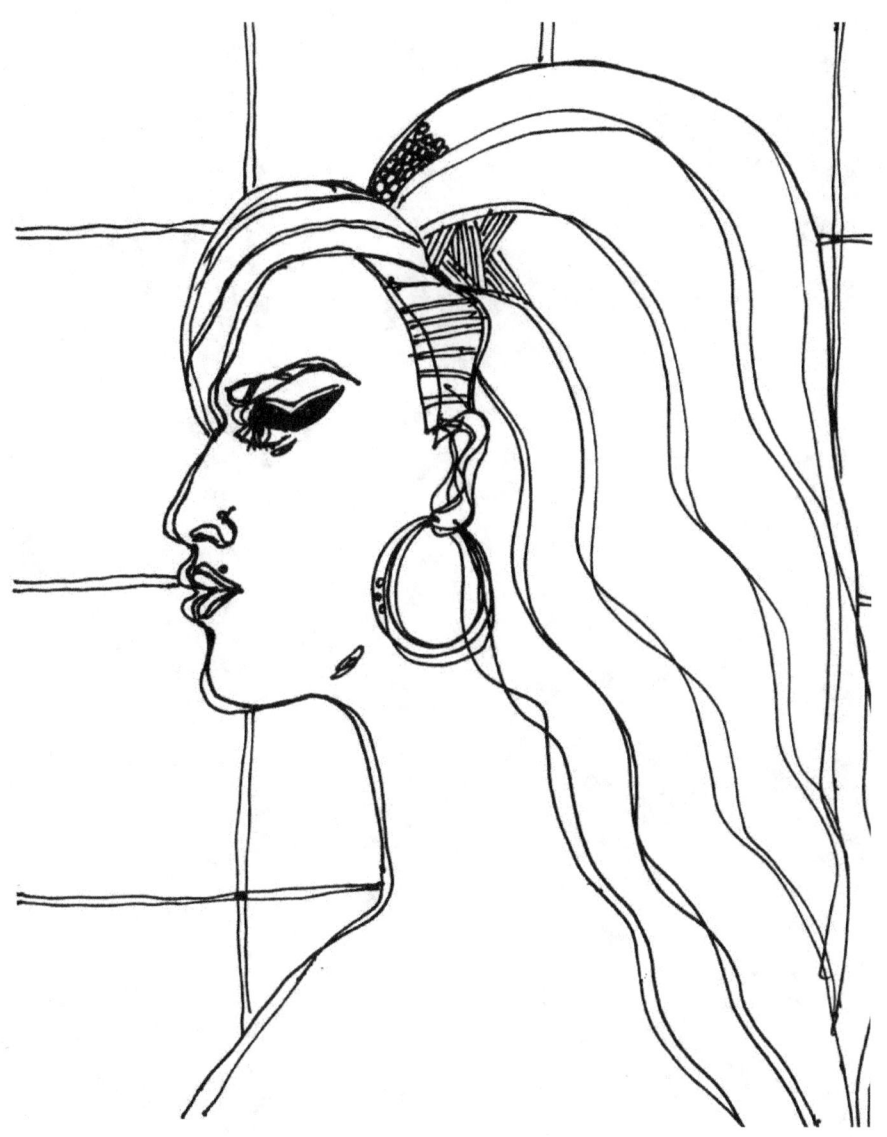

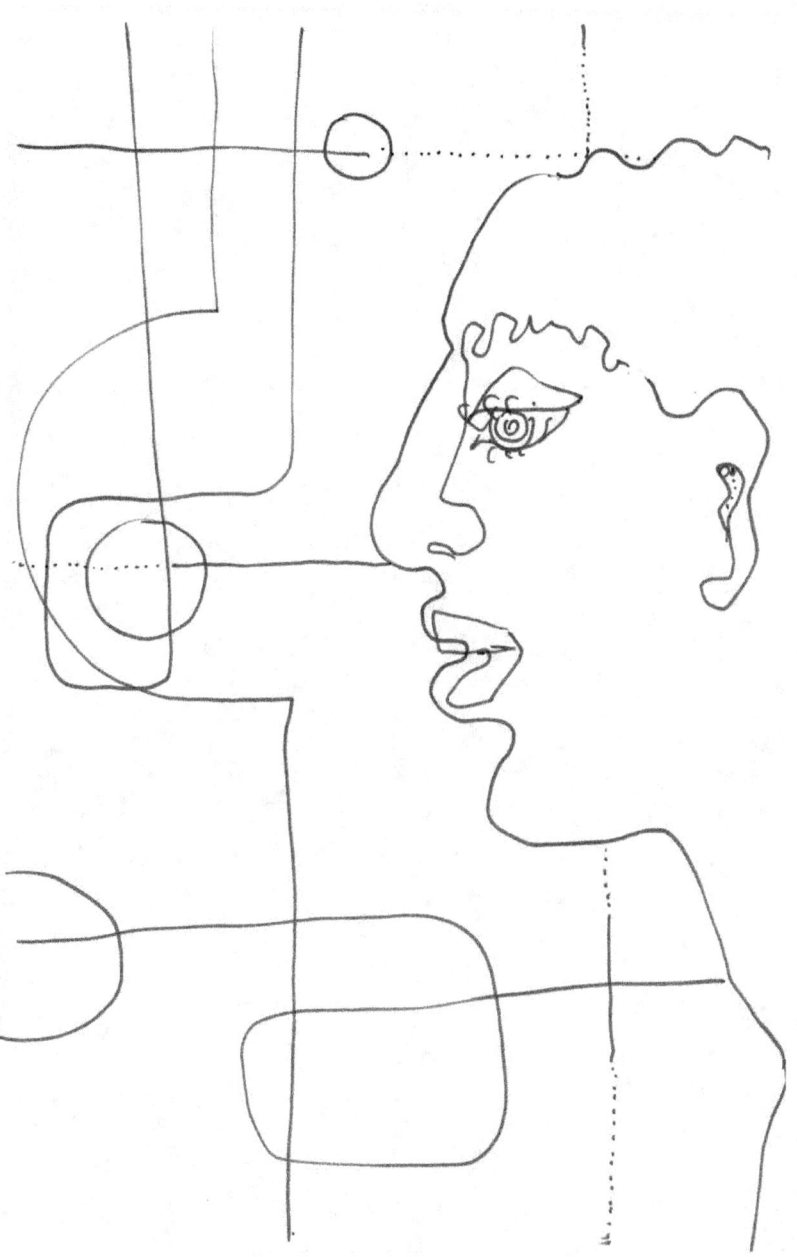

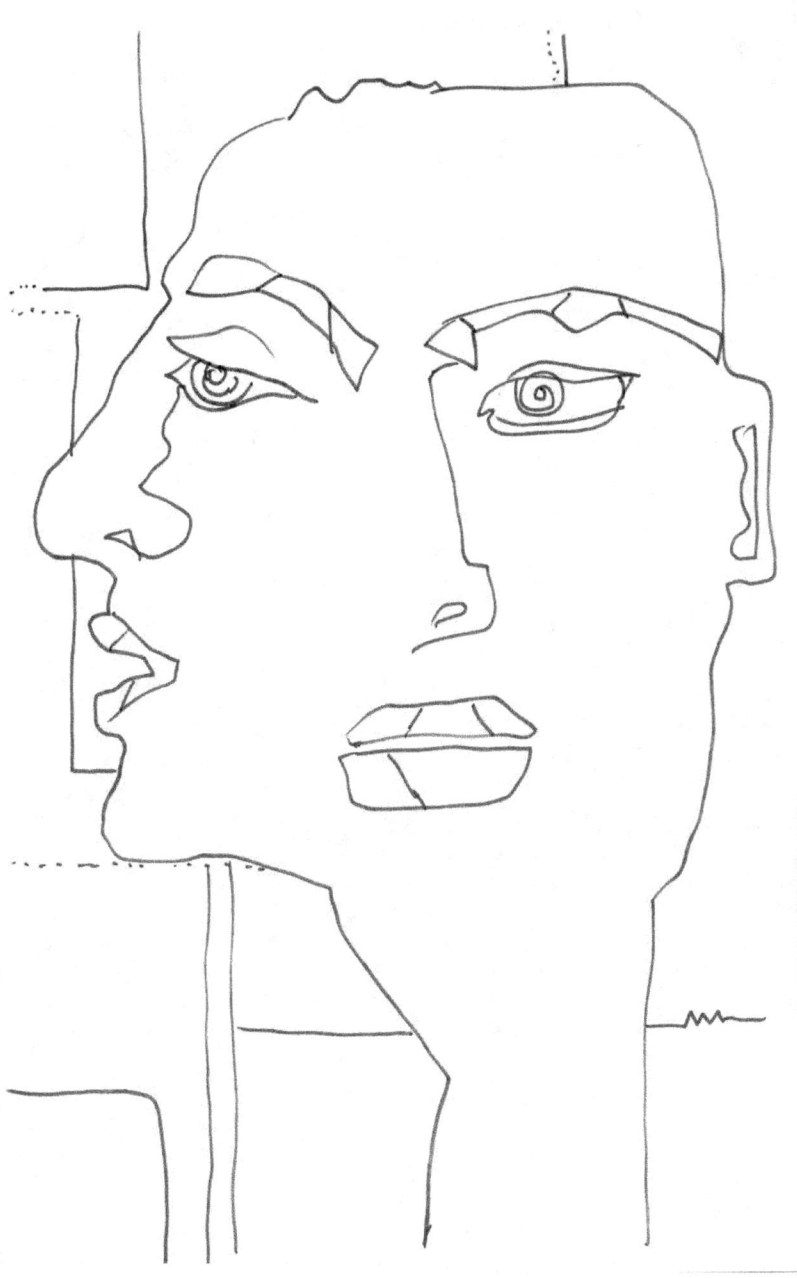

Improvise With Nadia Russ

Next pages invite you to improvise with the ink pen. The drawings are like music -
they can be happy, sad, mysterious, and straight forward. . . We draw our mood, the feelings, and people or things, which left the trace in our sub-consciousness.
The following pages offer the Nadia Russ' drawings for you not to copy them (they are copyrighted) but to examine them and to learn about the different variations and what you can do with the line and repetitive patterns. Eraser is never used because if a 'mistake' was made, the following repetitive patterns balance the whole composition.

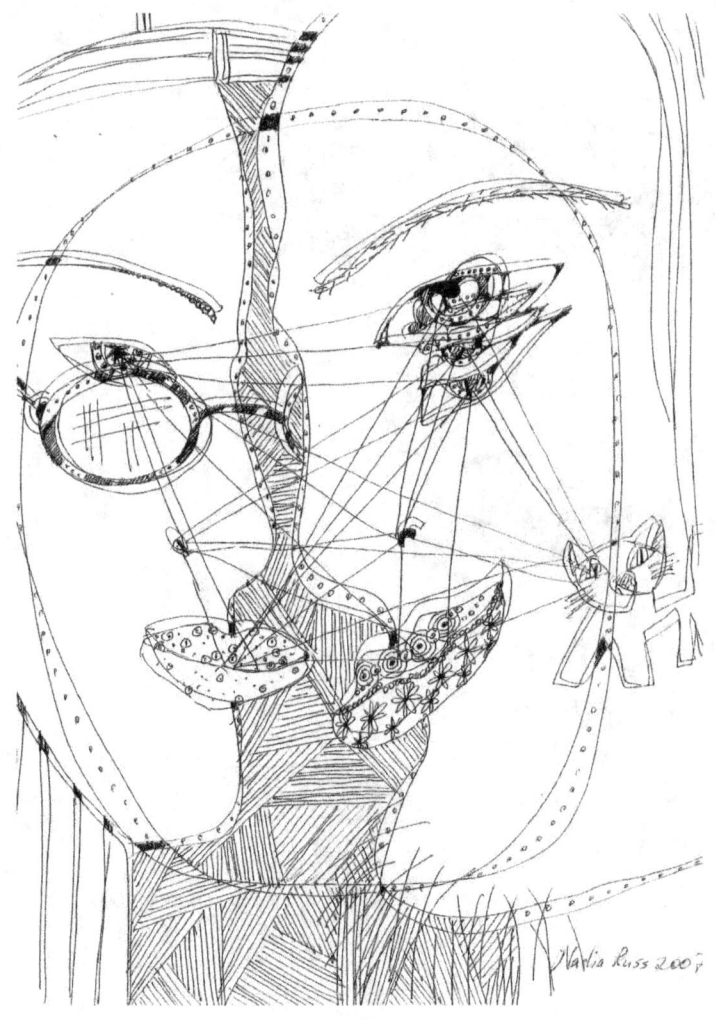

Nadia Russ, Faces 9, ink on paper, 2007

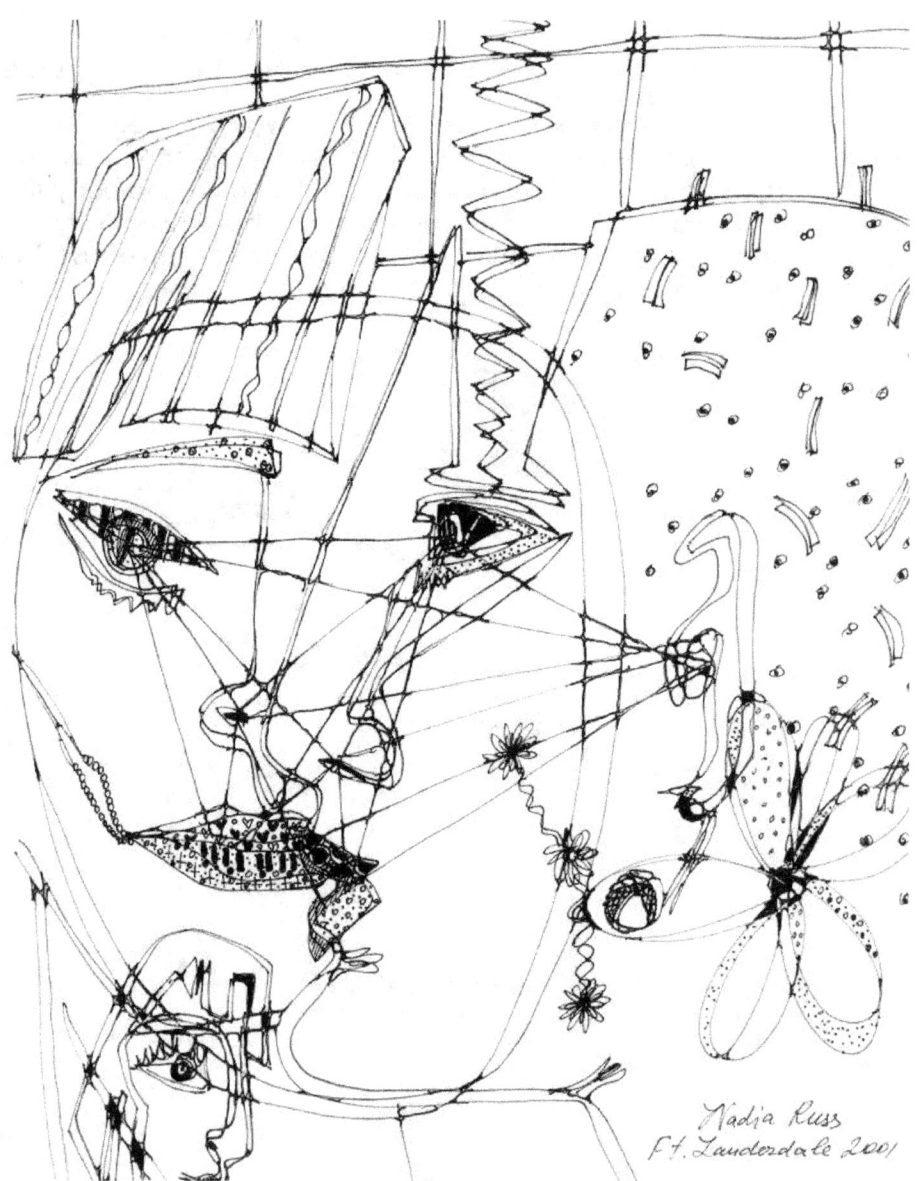

Nadia Russ, *Faces*, 8.5"x11", ink on paper, 2001

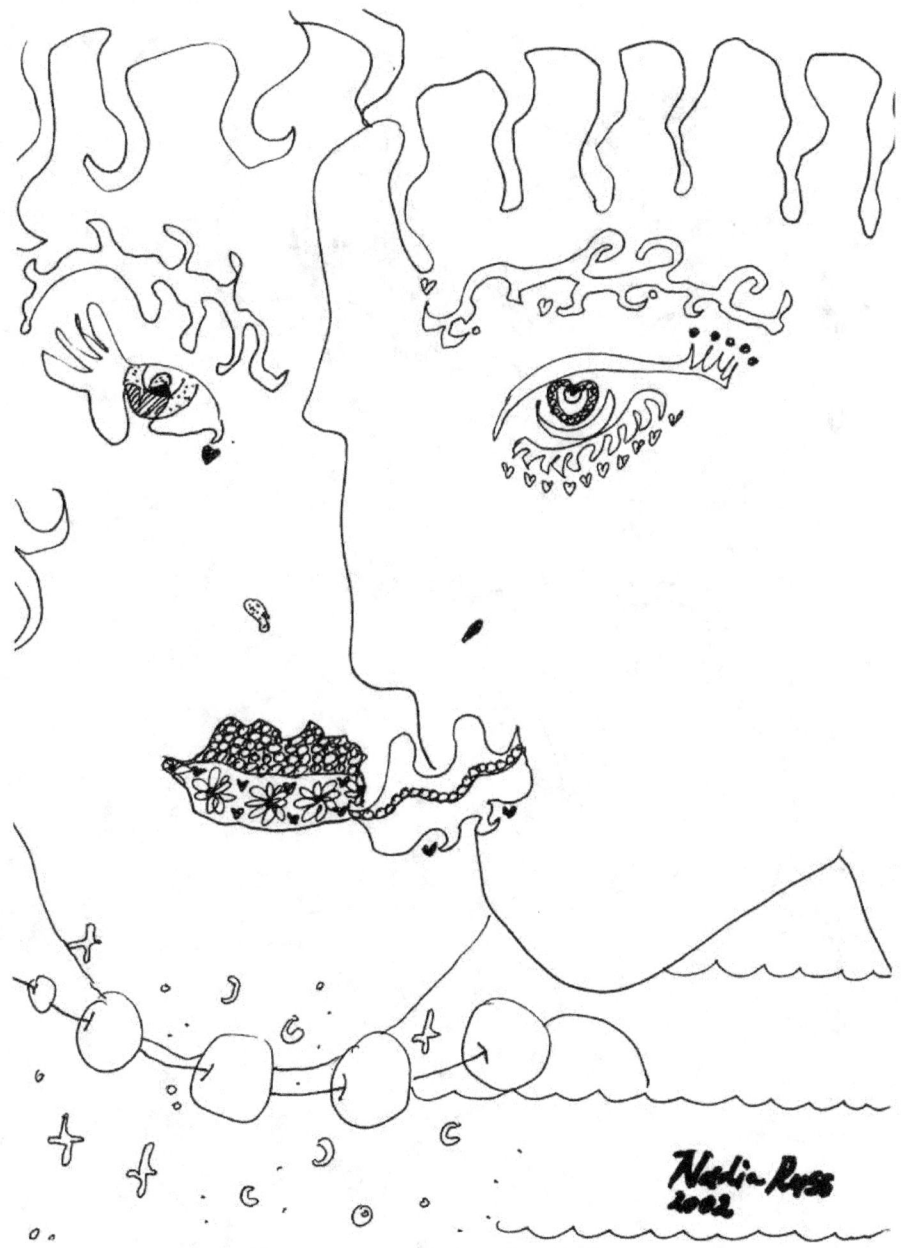

Nadia Russ, *Faces*, 7"x10", ink on paper, 2002

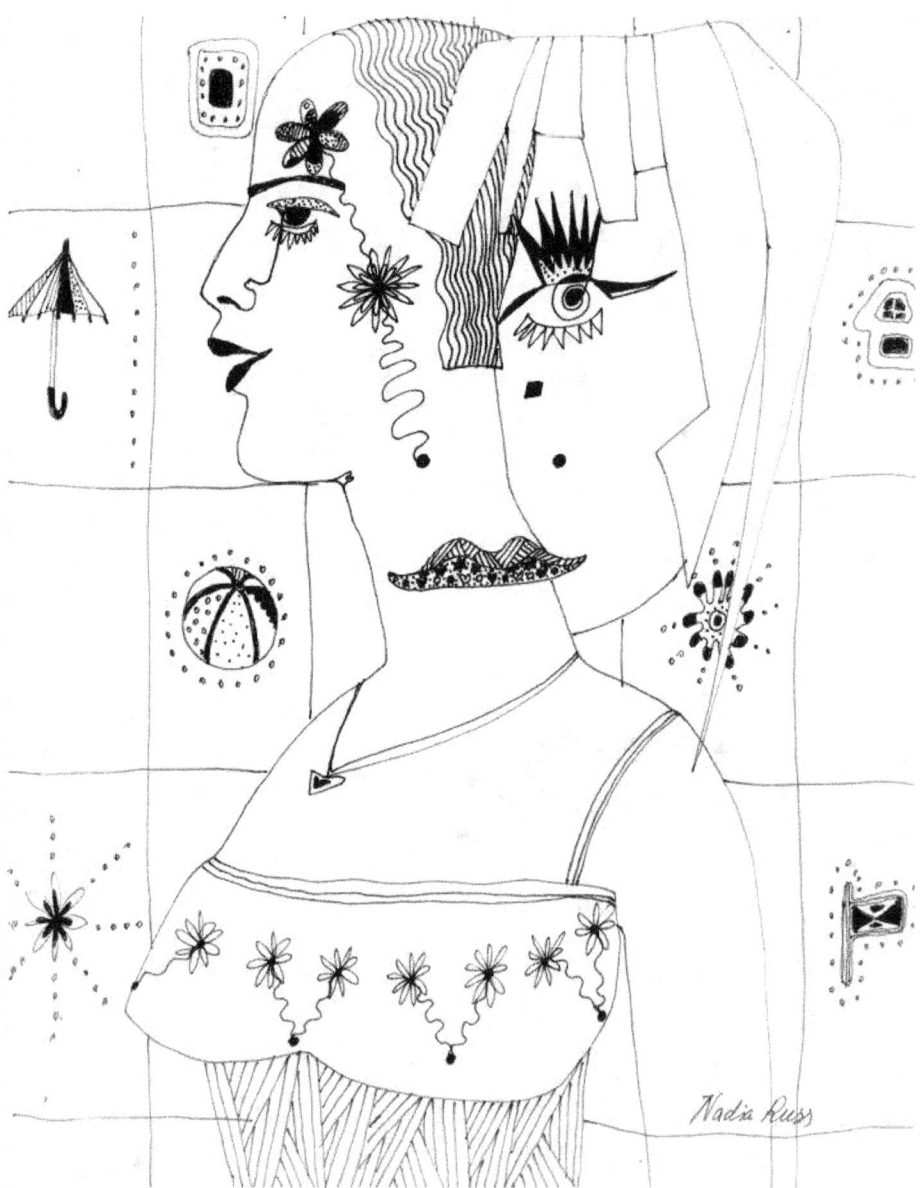

Nadia Russ, *Faces*, 8.5"x11", ink on paper, 2003

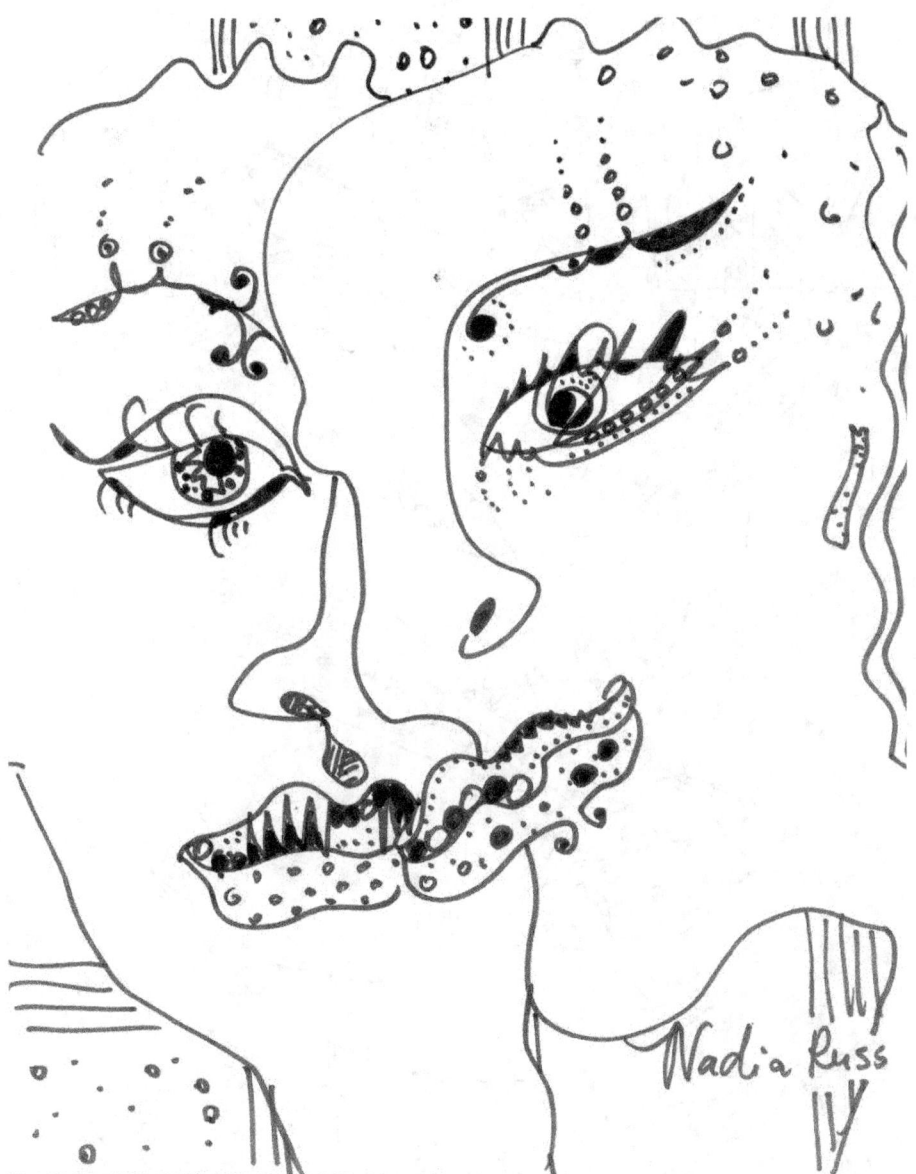

Nadia Russ, *Faces-203*, 8.5"x11", ink on paper, 2008

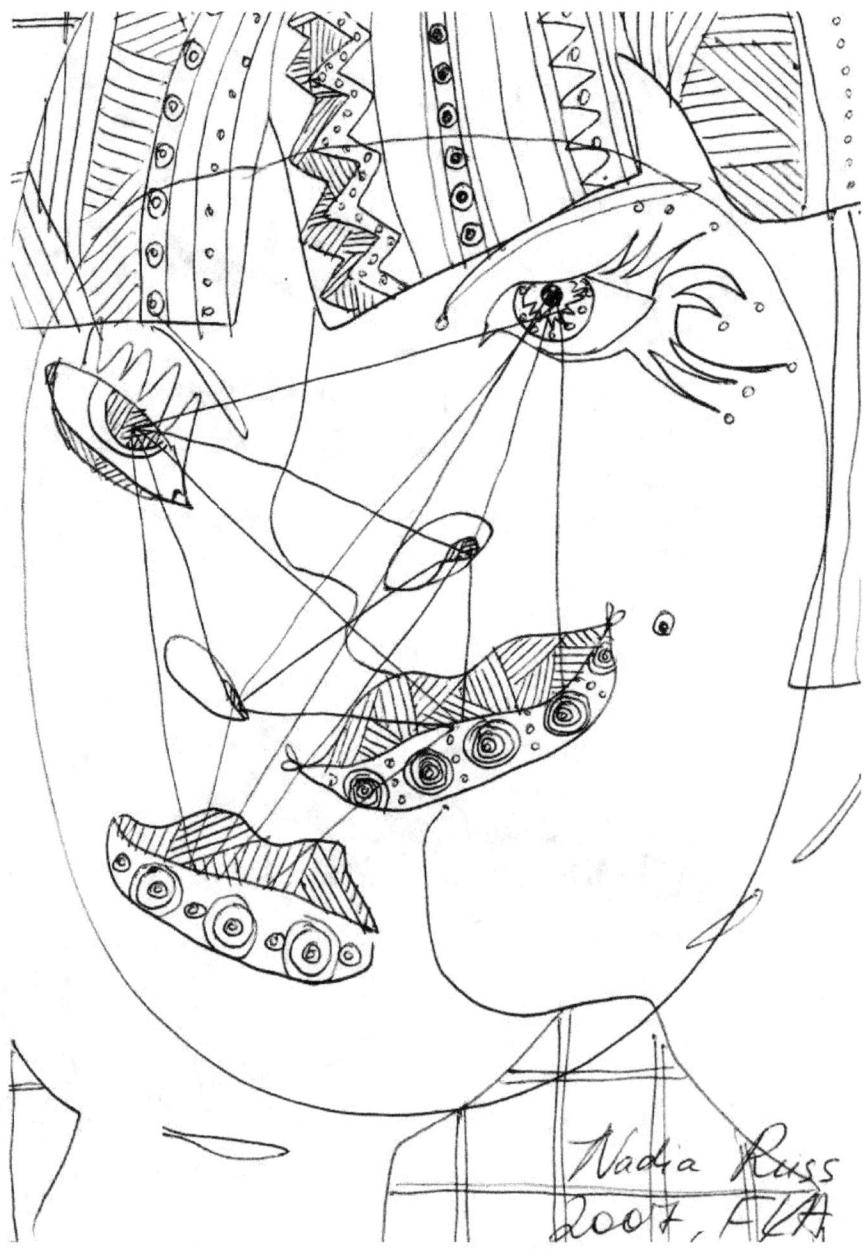

Nadia Russ, *Faces 1*, 4"x5.5", ink on paper, 2007

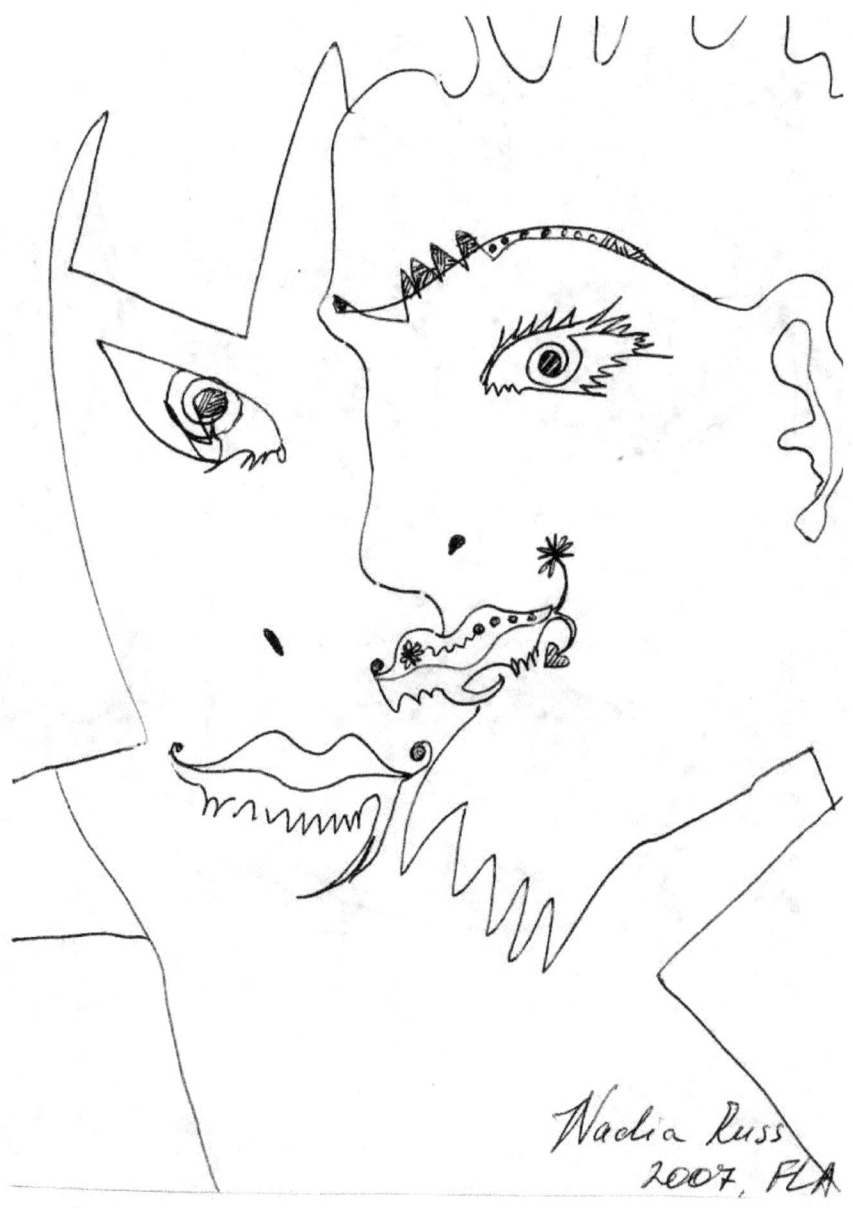

Nadia Russ, *Faces-4*, ink on paper, 4"x5.5", 2007

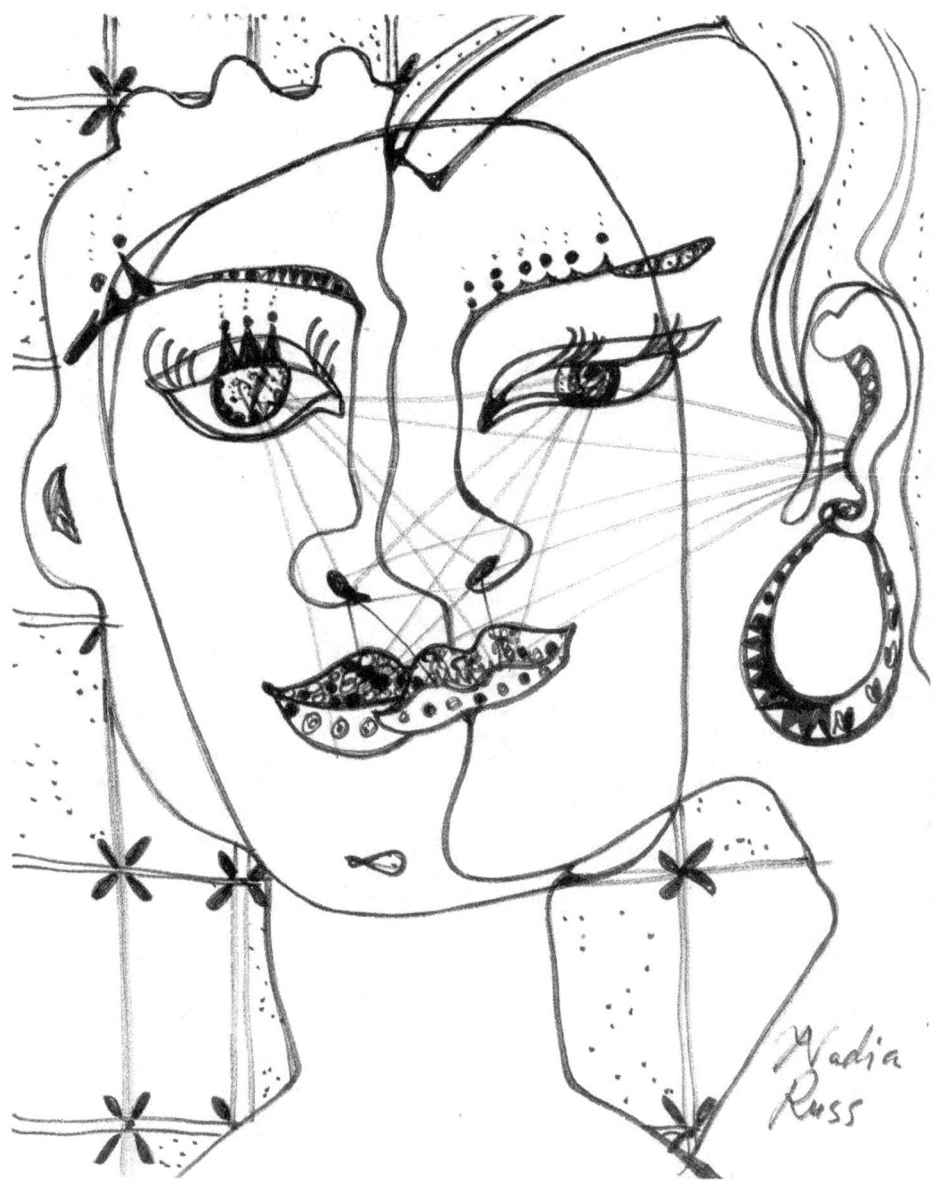

Nadia Russ, *Faces 213 NYC*, ink on paper, 8"x511" 2008

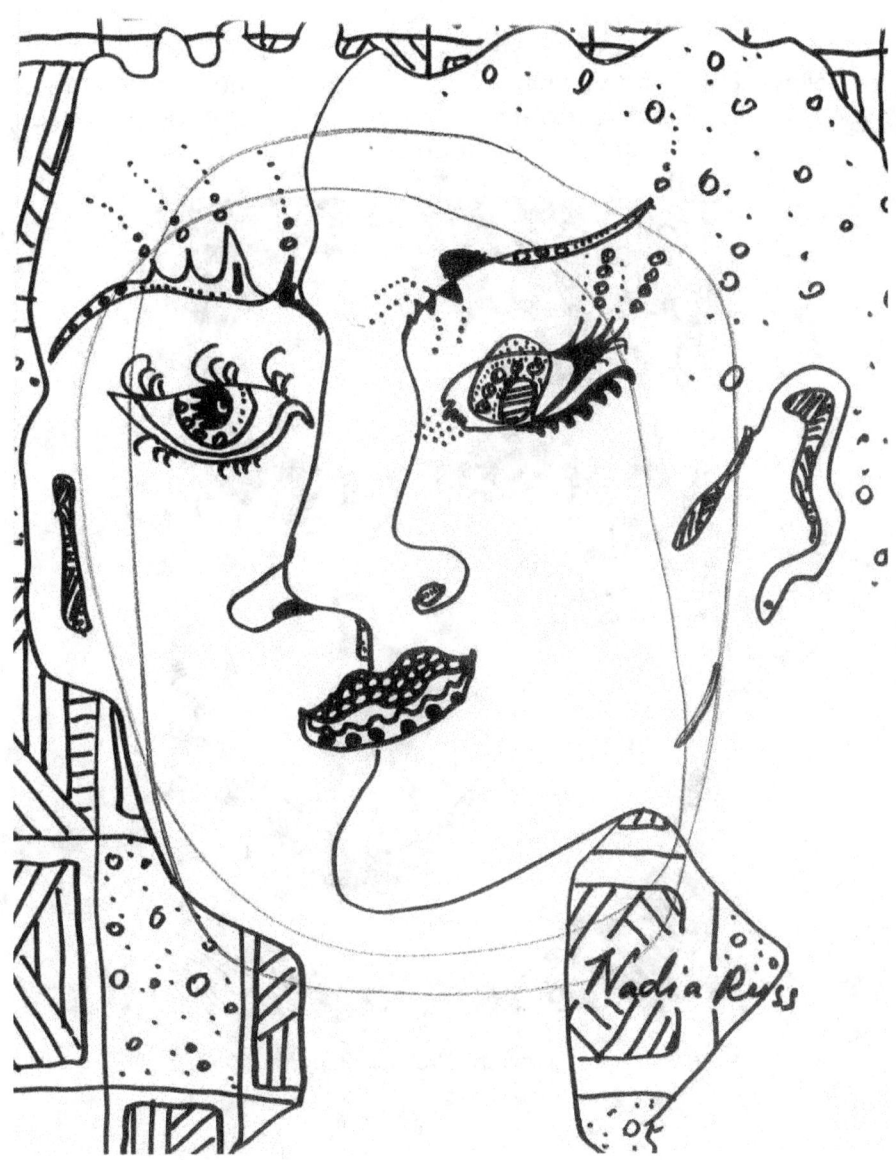

Nadia Russ, *Faces 208 NYC*, 8"x511", ink on paper, 2008

Use the following pages to draw NeoPopRealism ink images from the scratch. Improvise using the line and repetitive patterns, use your imagination, enjoy the process.

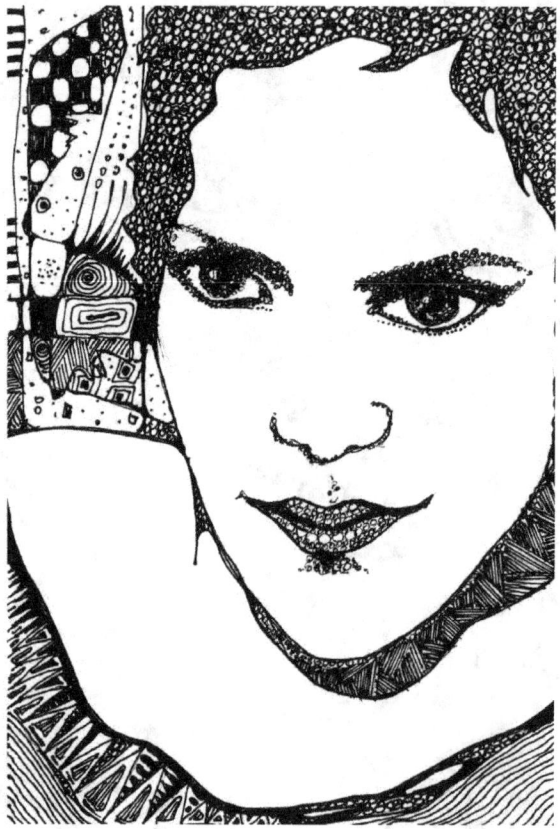

Nadia Russ, *A Woman*, 5"x8", ink on paper, 2011

Create your repetitive patterns Gallery

The following pages offer you to create your repetitive patterns Gallery. Fill each section with the different repetitive patterns using your imagination and artistic skills.

The drawing repetitive patterns is rewarding process, it helps you to relax, to recuperate, and to clear away stress hormones that may have built up. The drawing process occupies your mind, diverting it from the problems that are causing you stress.

Create patterns gallery using the line, circles, squares, ovals, triangles, rectangular; combine them. You can use these patterns later in your future ink drawings. Create, relax, and meditate.

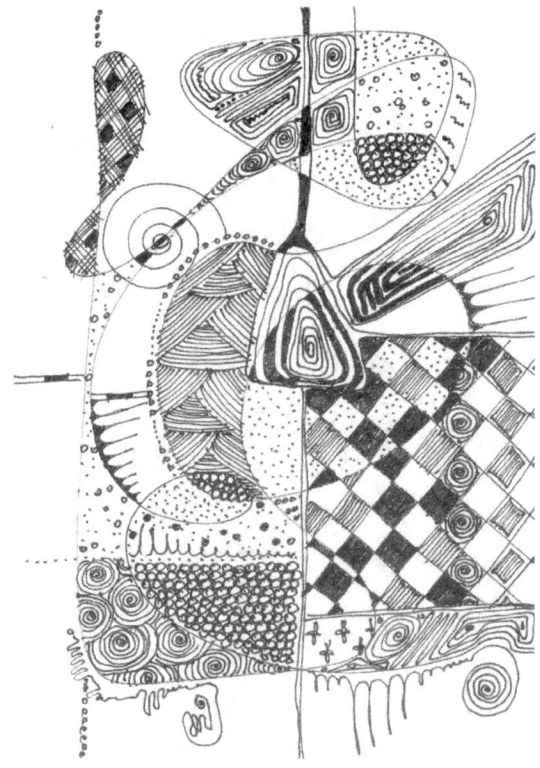

Nadia Russ, *Abstract*, ink on paper, 5"x8.5"

1	2	3
4	5	6
7	8	9
10	11	12

13	14	15
16	17	18
19	20	21
22	23	24

25	26	27
28	29	30
31	32	33
34	35	36

37	38	39
40	41	42
43	44	45
46	47	48

"People make the rules and break the rules, but harmony is eternal." Nadia Russ

Your exercising pages

The following four images are for you to complete them here and now. This is the abstract backgrounds for your realistic images (cars, faces, etc.) It is the skeleton, which needs some meat - the repetitive patterns. Complete these images the way you want; show what you have learned from this book. Follow the previous instructions and, no doubts, you will be able to get the wonderful result. The last pages of this book are for you to draw the realistic images with abstract backgrounds from the beginning to end. Enjoy the process!

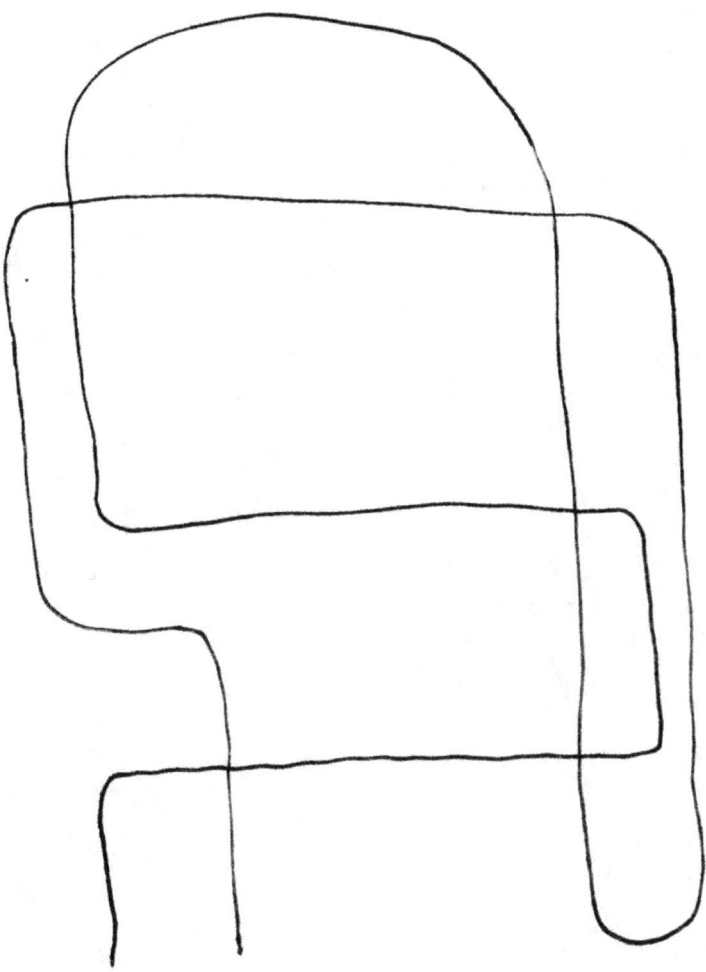

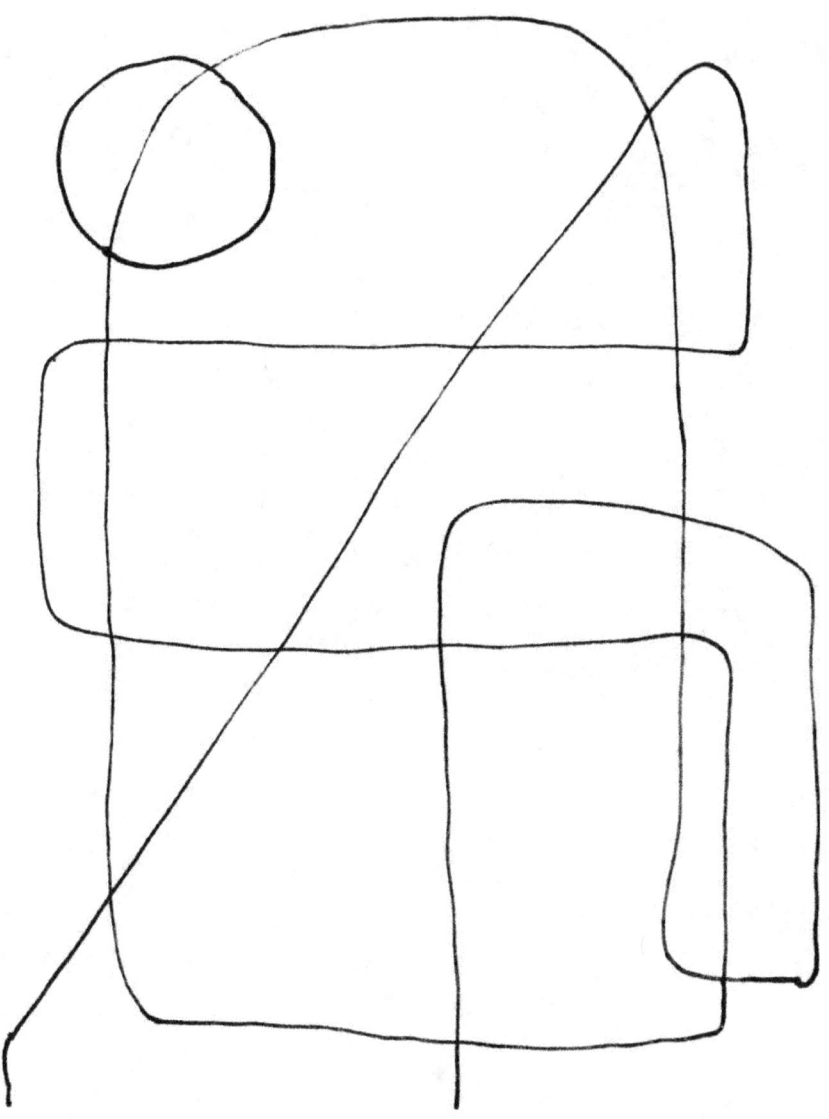

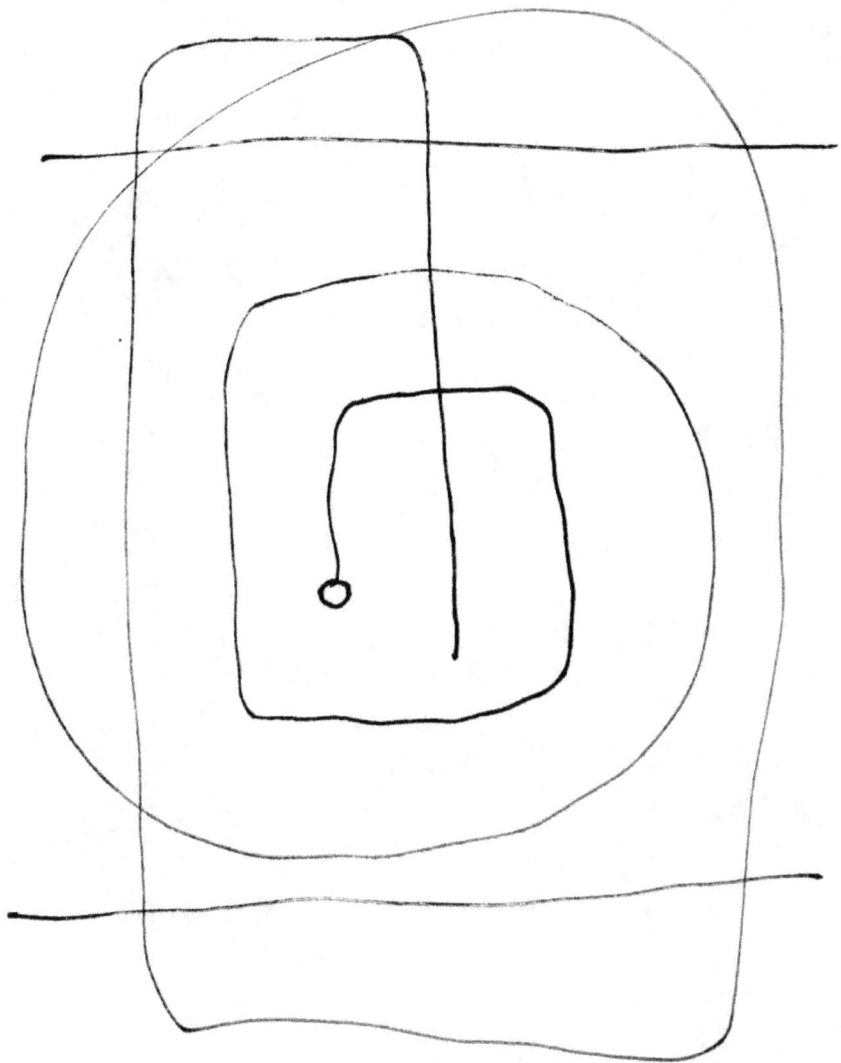

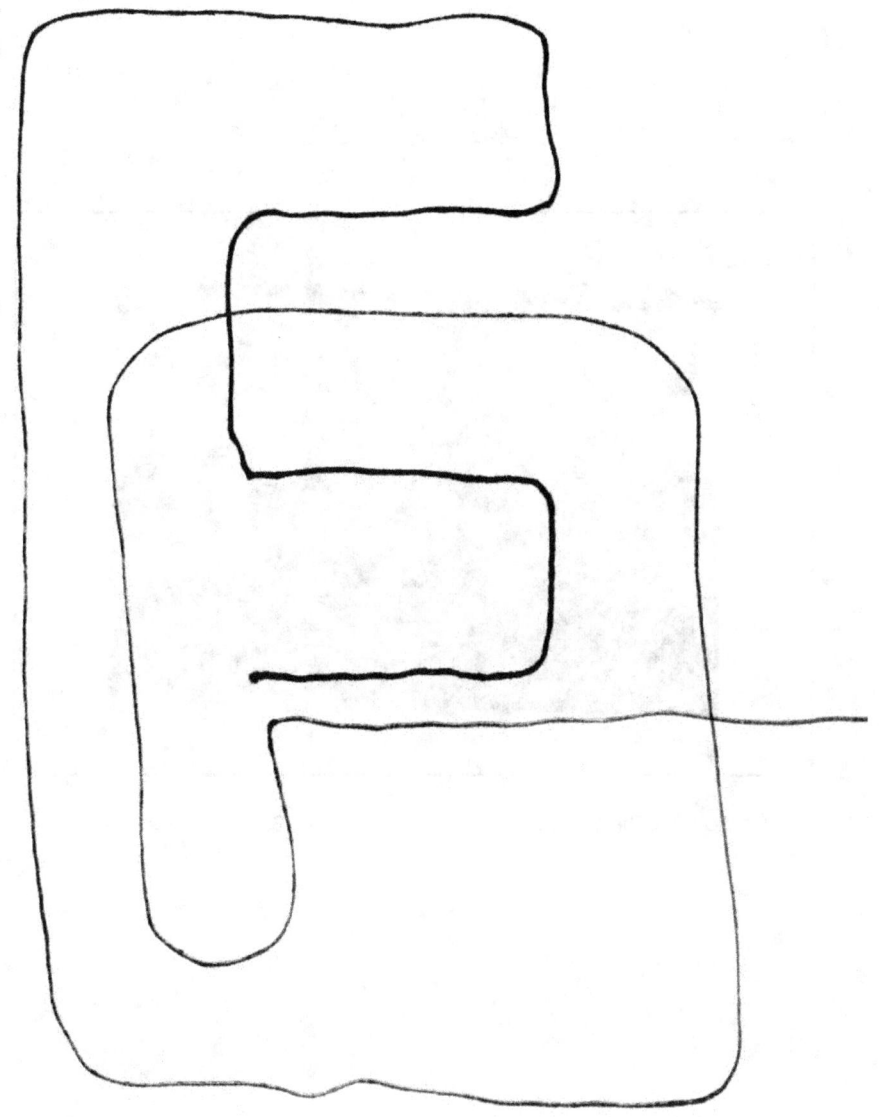

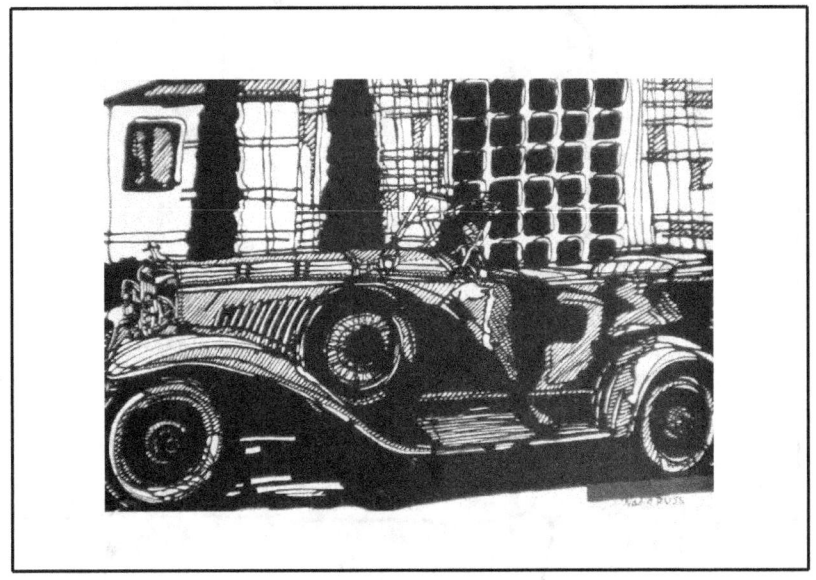

Nadia Russ, *The Classic Car*, ink on paper, 22"x26", 1997, Bahamas

About NeoPopRealism creator Nadia Russ

Nadia Russ (aka Nadejda Maloletneva) was born into a former professional military officer's family. As a child, she began studying art from famous masters of the past through art books and reproductions, which her mother Vera was collecting in their home. Nadia daily heard about and saw the reproductions of works of Leonardo da Vinci, Michelangelo, Rafael, contemporary Russian artists such as Petrov-Vodkin.

She began painting and drawing seriously in 1989. A few months later, her first ink drawings were exhibited in a group exhibition in famous Moscow's Manege and later, in other Moscow's art galleries. In 1992, she successfully showed her work in New York City.

In 1996-2000, Nadia resided in the Bahamas, where her work gained some special brightness. There, she got her pseudonym to her original 'Nadejda Maloletneva', which was easier to pronounce - 'Nadia Russ'. In 2000-2001, in Xanadu hotel, she operated her Art Gallery Club 13, where she exhibited her acrylic artworks on canvas.

In 2000, she moved to the United States, where she lives up until present. January 4, 2003, Nadia Russ created a word NeoPopRealism and manifested internationally new style of visual arts which combines the brightness and simplicity of Pop Art with deep and psychological realism and has graphic nature. Her artworks are in private and permanent public collections including MOYA - Museum of Young Art in Vienna (Austria), Simferopol and Sumy Art Museums in Ukraine, Kinsey Institute of Indiana University (USA), Ukrainian Museum in New York City (USA), WEAM - World Erotic Art Museum in Miami (USA), Schacknow Museum of Fine Arts (USA), Historical Museum of Fort Lauderdale (USA), Lebedyn and Konotop Art Museums (Ukraine), D. Burliuk Foundation (Ukraine), and other.

In 2008-2010, Nadia Russ founded and juried Int'l NeoPopRealism Starz Art competitions. She authored a few art-related books such as "NeoPopRealism Starz: 21st Century ART" two volumes, "New Millennium ART", "Fort Lauderdale 100: A Must-Have Collector's Edition." She is the founder (2007) of the *NeoPopRealism Journal & Wonderpedia*, publications online, dedicated to arts, culture, books, news, celebrities and more. Nadia Russ lives in New York City and Florida. Visit her website at www.nadiaruss.com.

Conclusion

W hat is Art?

Now, when you have learned how to draw the NeoPopRealism ink images, you might have your answer to this open question. We'd be happy to hear from you, e-mail us to neopoprealismpress@mail.com. Also, if you have a blog, post there the images of your NeoPopRealism ink drawings and a story how you learned to draw them. Have a wonderful journey to the world of NeoPopRealism!

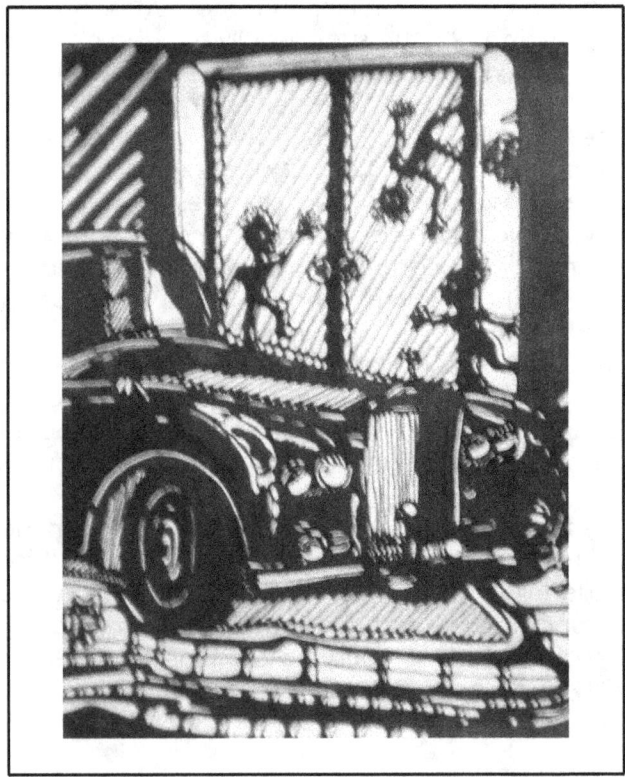

Nadia Russ, *Mysterious Door*, ink on paper, 22"x26", 1997, Bahamas

NeoPopRealism ten canons for happier life

1. Be beautiful.

2. Be creative and productive; never stop studying and learning.

3. Be peace-loving, positive-minded.

4. Do not accept communism or any totalitarian philosophy.

5. Be free-minded, do the best you can to move the world to peace and harmony.

6. Be family oriented, self-disciplined.

7. Be free spirited. Follow your dreams, if they are not destructive, but constructive.

8. Believe in god. God is one; it is harmony and striving for perfection.

9. Be supportive to those who need you, be generous.

10. Create your life as a great adventurous story.

Created by Nadia Russ in 2004

Additional books - teaching / learning material on NeoPopRealism Ink drawing
for adults, teenagers and children

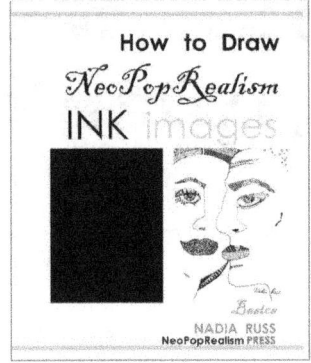

ISBN: 9780615515755
FOR TEENS & ADULTS

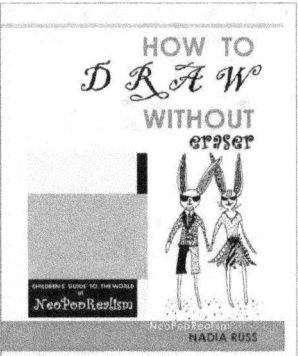

ISBN: 9780615521824
FOR CHILDREN

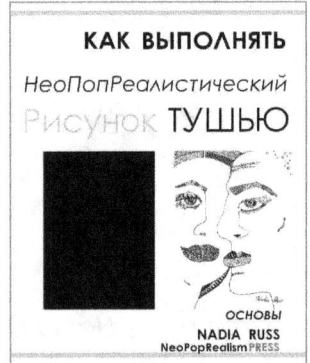

"How to Draw NeoPopRealism Ink Images:
Basics."
Russian translation.
ISBN: 9780615516967

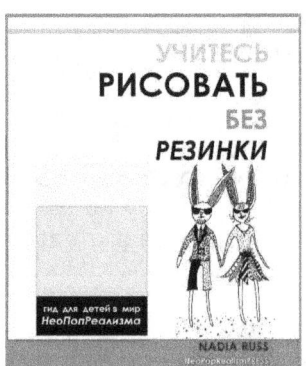

"How to Draw Without Eraser:
Russian translation

ISBN: 9780615523484

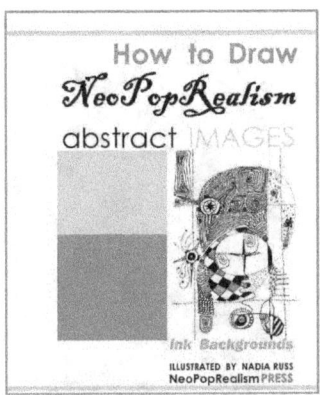

ISBN: 9780615527437
FOR TEENS & ADULTS

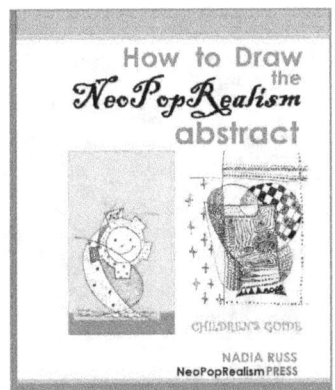

ISBN: 9780615545332
FOR CHILDREN

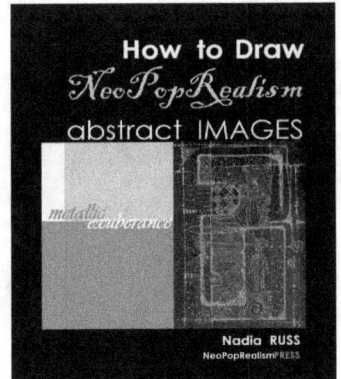

ISBN: 9780615560991
FOR TEENS AND ADULTS

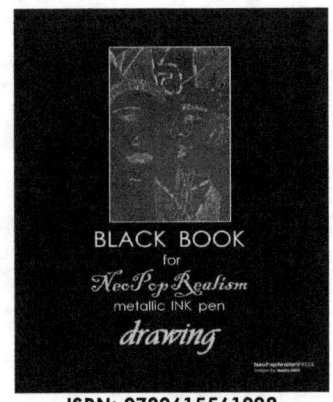

ISBN: 9780615561028
FOR TEENS AND ADULT

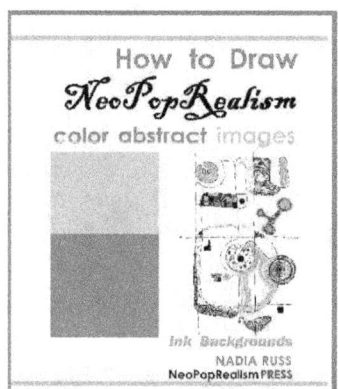

ISBN: 9780615581804
FOR TEENS AND ADULTS

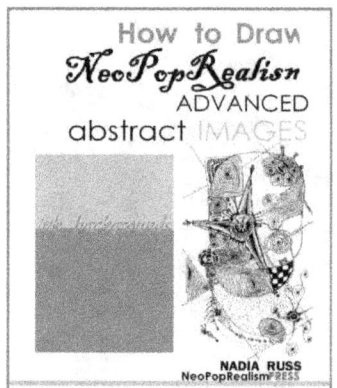

ISBN: 9780615592558
FOR TEENS AND ADULTS

www.ingramcontent.com/pod-product-compliance
Lightning Source LLC
Chambersburg PA
CBHW081118180526
45170CB00008B/2895